Knitting Knee-Highs
Sock Styles from Classic to Contemporary

Barb Brown

KRAUSE PUBLICATIONS
CINCINNATI, OHIO

www.fwmedia.com

15 14 13 12 11   5 4 3 2 1

DISTRIBUTED IN CANADA BY FRASER DIRECT
100 Armstrong Avenue
Georgetown, ON, Canada L7G 5S4
Tel: (905) 877-4411

DISTRIBUTED IN THE U.K. AND EUROPE BY F+W MEDIA
INTERNATIONAL
Brunel House, Newton Abbot, Devon, TQ12 4PU, England
Tel: (+44) 1626 323200, Fax: (+44) 1626 323319
Email: postmaster@davidandcharles.co.uk

DISTRIBUTED IN AUSTRALIA BY CAPRICORN LINK
P.O. Box 704, S. Windsor NSW, 2756 Australia
Tel: (02) 4577-3555

Library of Congress Cataloging in Publication Data
Brown, Barb
  Knitting knee-highs : sock styles from classic to contemporary / Barb Brown.
    p. cm.
  Includes index.
  ISBN 978-1-4402-1369-4 (alk. paper)
  1. Socks. 2. Knitting. I. Title.
  TT825.B758 2011
  746.43'2--dc22
                    2010035810

Editor: Jennifer Claydon
Designer: Corrie Schaffeld
Production coordinator: Greg Nock
Illustrator: Karen Manthey
Photographer: Ric Deliantoni
Stylist: Monica Skrzelowski
Makeup artists: Cass Brake and Nicole Deitsch

F+W Media, Inc. would like to
thank Baker Hunt Art and Cultural Center
for generously sharing the beautiful
location shown in this book.

Metric Conversion Chart		
To convert	to	multiply by
Inches	Centimeters	2.54
Centimeters	Inches	0.4
Feet	Centimeters	30.5
Centimeters	Feet	0.03
Yards	Meters	0.9
Meters	Yards	1.1

Dedication

This book is dedicated to Margrethe Elisabeth (Colvin) Wolczuk and Samuel Wolczuk, who raised me to believe I could do it. And to Carol Sulcoski, who showed me how to do it. And to Eric Thompson and Omar Farooq, who made sure I was here to do it.

But most of all, to Glenn, my best friend, who put up with me while I did it.

Acknowledgments

With special thanks to the generous volunteers who knit their fingers to the bone helping with all the samples:
    Janet Anderson, Lynne Anderson, Jennifer Carter-Morgan, Wendy Cheung, Mary Alyce Heaton, Birgit Hoeger, Caroline Hyndman, Karen Klute, Julie Malin, Trisha Paetsch, Jenni Reiz, Virginia Sattler-Reimer, Marg Sjostrom, Kirsten Snider, Caroline Sommerfeld, Kim Whitley and Katherine Wowk.

And to:
    Celeigh Wool of Millet, Alberta and Wool Revival of Edmonton, Alberta for letting me shamelessly use their shops for a meeting place, and allowing me to raid their stock in emergencies.

About the Author

Barb Brown is a designer and life-long knitter living in Alberta, Canada. She is also the owner of Wild Geese Fibres, an online business specializing in natural fibre yarns and spinning fibre.
    She teaches knitting, designing and dye workshops at yarn shops and community colleges.
    Barb's designs have appeared in *Vogue Knitting*, *Yarn Forward*, *A Needle Pulling Thread*, and *Twists and Turns*, as well as in the book *Knitting Socks with Handpainted Yarn* by Carol Sulkoski (Interweave).

Table *of* Contents

Introduction

Many people look at a pair of hand-knit knee-highs and, while they love the look of them and would dearly like to own a pair, are frightened off by the amount of knitting that seems to be required. However, there really isn't a lot more knitting involved in a pair of knee-highs than there is in a pair of socks. Think about it: The leg on a pair of ladies' socks is usually between seven and nine inches. The leg on a pair of knee-highs is only around thirteen inches. That is a difference of just four to six inches. If you were knitting the sleeve of a sweater, you'd barely be started! For a little bit of extra knitting you get an awful lot of satisfaction.

Knee-highs are the perfect garment for showcasing your skills and trying out a new technique. You may never have knit lace although you love the look of it. A sweater or shawl can be daunting: So many stitches! So many rows! But in the time it takes to knit a pair of knee-highs you can master a new technique, and you will have knit enough to know whether it is something you want to do again (or if you would rather cross the Himalayas on a yak in winter wearing only a bathing suit). Either way, you will own a garment to be proud of.

Socks are great for this as well, of course, but don't look nearly as spectacular. Imagine attending your next knitting group or fiber festival wearing perfectly knit knee-highs. Quite often fiber-related events are held in the warm weather, when a sweater would be too hot to even contemplate. Knee-highs with a skirt, shorts or capris are just perfect!

In days gone by people attending festivals wore their very best clothing, including beautiful and complex hand-knit stockings. A bride knit them for her wedding, and for her husband. Knitters did their best work on these special pairs, showcasing their skills. Family members and sweethearts alike wore them with pride. Even after cheap machine-made socks could be easily bought, the fancy work still came out to play on special days.

Modern times and customs gradually spread, and many people stopped these traditions. These beautiful garments languished at the bottom of trunks and the back of drawers. Fortunately, interest in these arts has revived, and become stylish once more. Knitters can again be a part of these traditions.

Knit knee-highs for yourself, your family or your friends. Knit a pair of kilt hose, even if you don't wear a kilt. Do you have a secret longing to wear something wild and crazy, or frilly and lacy? Frivolous knee-highs hidden under slacks or jeans are a harmless secret vice.

Some people worry about wearing out a pair of knee-highs and dread the holes that will appear in the feet (as they are bound to do). All that work, all those hours, and now they are unwearable! If, like me, you consider the term "darning socks" to mean holding them over the garbage can, saying "darn socks" and tossing them in, think about this: Run a strand of smooth contrasting yarn in and out through the stitches above the heel to mark a straight line. Now gather your courage and cut the foot off just under this line. Pick up the live stitches, knit some ribbing and you have a pair of lovely, fitted legwarmers. Or, after cutting the feet off, pick up the live stitches and knit new feet in a complimentary or contrasting yarn. For very little effort, your knee-highs will have a new life and all that work won't be wasted.

Knitters also worry about fitting knee-highs to their legs. Included in this book is a general formula to help you decide which size is right for your leg. The human body is based on percentages: If you know what size sock fits your foot properly, your leg measurements are likely directly related to this, which takes a lot of guesswork out of sizing.

So, gather your knitting needles and yarn (and your courage, if needed) and give knitting knee-highs a try!

Getting Started

Inside this brief chapter there is a plethora of information about knitting knee-highs. Over the next several pages you'll learn about making knee-highs, fitting knee-highs and converting patterns from sock to knee-high and from knee-high to several different sock styles.

If you have never knit a pair of knee-highs for yourself, I recommend knitting a pair from the formula on page 12. If you knit stripes as suggested, you will have a very handy reference; in fact you will have a pattern right there on your legs! Any adjustments you make can be easily tracked by the stripes.

You'll find a lot of information in this chapter, but if you're too excited about the patterns in the next chapter to pause here and learn more, let me send you forward with these words of advice: Knit a swatch in the round to get an accurate stitch count, and also to check that you have some stretch to the fabric at the gauge you are getting. Use sufficiently long needles. The ones you normally use to knit socks just might not be long enough to hold the large number of stitches at the top of a knee-high. There is nothing worse than having the end stitches pop off and unravel. Swatch, swatch, swatch! Especially for colorwork patterns. And remember, while a firm fabric is desirable, it must have stretch. If you aren't sure of the leg length for a pair you are knitting as a gift, try knitting the ribbing at the top extra long. The recipient can then roll the top down for a cuff. You can make a note of how much roll back there is for the next pair you knit for them.

Did I mention you really should swatch?

Knee-High Formula

You can use this formula, along with a few measurements, to create your own custom-fit knee-highs. Or, having knit a few pairs of knee-highs, you may wish to try converting your favorite sock pattern into a knee-high. This formula can help you with that as well.

If you are converting a sock pattern you're familiar with, you can use the stitch counts from the pattern as a starting point. If, however, you are creating your own pattern from scratch, you'll need to start with your foot measurement and your knitting gauge.

Usually, the most comfortable pair of socks you own will be ½" (1.5cm) or so smaller in circumference than your actual foot measurement. If you aren't sure how wide to make the foot of your knee-high, take out a pair of socks that fit your feet nicely. (Commercial socks will work, as long as they don't have a stretchy rib-style foot.) Measure the width. Using the measurement of a pair of socks, rather than your foot measurement, gives a much more accurate result.

In general, the circumference of a person's calf is a percentage of the circumference of their foot. The length of the leg is also an average percentage of this number. Instead of using measurments, you can also measure your leg and work from there. If you do, get another person to measure your leg. Measuring your own leg accurately is not easy, even if you are a yoga expert. It is very difficult to read the measuring tape when your head is upside down and your foot is somewhere near your ear.

Of course, this formula is based on averages, so it is a good plan to check the numbers against actual measurements. Average is just that, the highest and the lowest measurements with the inbetweens, all divided up. So, on average, no one is really average! If you find that regular-length pants are either too long or too short, then, like most of us, you are outside the "average." If you buy "tall" pants, increase the length of your knee-highs by five percent. If you fit "petite" sizing, reduce the length by five percent. If you are considering knitting a pair of knee-highs as a gift, and know the recipient's foot size, this formula is a good place to start.

Step 1

If you are converting a sock pattern to a knee-high, choose the size that will fit your foot circumference (remember to allow for negative ease [see page 15]; approximately 10% for regular patterns or 5% for stranded and heavy yarn). Check the pattern for the number of stitches in the foot or ankle.

If you are starting from scratch, multiply the desired foot circumference for your knee-high by your stitch gauge to produce the number of stitches for the foot of your sock.

Example One: 72 stitches

Example Two: 64 stitches

Step 2

Multiply the number of stitches by ⅓ to find the number of stitches to cast on for your knee-highs.

Example One: 72 × ⅓ = 96

Example Two: 64 × ⅓ = 86 (rounded up)

Step 3

Multiply the number of foot stitches (not cast-on stitches) by ⅓. Knit this number of rounds of ribbing to start the knee-high. This will produce a ribbing that is fairly long, which gives some leeway if the total length is a little too long, as it can be folded over.

Example One: 72 × ⅓ = 24 rounds

Example Two: 64 × ⅓ = 22 rounds (rounded up)

For Women's sizes, take 75% of the above number for the correct number of rounds. The adjustment made for Women's sizes assumes that the average woman's leg is shorter than the average man's.

Example One: 24 × 75% = 18 rounds

Example Two: 22 × 75% = 16 rounds (rounded down)

Step 4

Multiply the number of cast-on stitches by ½; work that number of rounds with no shaping.

Example One: 96 × ½ = 48. Knit 48 rounds with no shaping.

Example Two: 86 × ½ = 43. Knit 43 rounds with no shaping.

For Women's sizes, take 75% of this number.

Example One: 48 × 75% = 36. Knit 36 rounds with no shaping.

Example Two: 43 × 75% = 32 (rounded down). Knit 32 rounds with no shaping.

Step 5

Follow the next several steps to calculate the calf decreases for your knee-highs.

A. Decreases will be done over the same number of rounds as the number of stitches in the foot.

Example One: 72 rounds

Example Two: 64 rounds

For Women's sizes, take 75% of this number.

Example One: 72 × 75% = 54 rounds

Example Two: 64 × 75% = 48 rounds

B. Subtract the number of stitches in the foot from the number of stitches cast on to calculate the number of decreases to work.

Example One: 96 - 72 = 24 stitches to decrease

Example Two: 86 - 64 = 22 stitches to decrease

C. Divide the number of stitches to be decreased by 2 (assuming 2 stitches will be decreased each decrease round) to give the number of decrease rounds to be worked.

Example One: 24 / 2 = 12 decrease rounds

Example Two: 22 / 2 = 11 decrease rounds

D. Divide the total rounds decreases are to be worked over (A) by the number of decrease rounds (C).

Example One: 72 / 12 = 6

Example Two: 64 / 11 = 6 (rounded up)

For Women's sizes

Example One: 54 / 12 = 5 (rounded up)

Example Two: 48 / 11 = 5 (rounded up)

E. Decrease on the next round, then every X rounds (the number calculated from D) for the number of times from C - 1.

Example One: every 6 rounds, 12 − 1 = 11 times (11 × 6 = 66 plus the 6 after the first round of decreases = 72 rounds)

Example Two: every 6 rounds, 11 − 1 = 10 times (10 × 6 = 60 plus the 6 after the first round of decreases = 66 rounds)

While you are creating your first pair of formula knee-highs, I suggest adding stripes to track your pattern: At each point that a shaping round is worked, knit that round in a contrasting color. If you also do this on the first round of the heel flap and the beginning of the toe shaping, you not only have a unique pair of leg coverings, but you also have a pair of knee-highs that functions as a portable pattern.

Step 6

Divide the number of stitches in the foot by 2, and work this many rounds plain.

Example One: 72 / 2 = 36

Example Two: 64 / 2 = 32

For Women's sizes, take 75% of this number.

Example One: 36 × 75% = 27

Example Two: 32 × 75% = 24

To finish, divide for the heel and proceed as you would for any sock.

Shoe Sizes	Women's Shoe Sizes				Men's Shoe Sizes			
If you are knitting a pair of knee-highs or socks as a gift, use this chart to help size them correctly.	US/CDN	UK	EU	Length	US/CDN	UK	EU	Length
	5	3	35	8.42" (21.6cm)	7	6	40	9.56" (24.5cm)
	5½	3½	35.5	8.58" (22cm)	7½	6½	40.5	9.75" (25cm)
	6	4	36	8.74" (22.4cm)	8	7	41	9.91" (25.4cm)
	6½	4½	36.5	8.89" (22.8cm)	8½	7½	41.5	10.06" (25.8cm)
	7	5	37	9.05" (23.2cm)	9	8	42	10.30" (26.4cm)
	7½	5½	37.5	9.24" (23.7cm)	9½	8½	42.5	10.41" (26.7cm)
	8	6	38	9.40" (24.1cm)	10	9	43	10.57" (27.1cm)
	8½	6½	38.5	9.56" (24.5cm)	10½	9½	43.5	10.73" (27.5cm)
	9	7	39	9.71" (24.9cm)	11	10	44	10.88" (27.9cm)
	9½	7½	39.5	9.95" (25.5cm)	11½	10½	44.5	11.08" (28.4cm)
	10	8	40	10.06" (25.8cm)	12	11	45	11.23" (28.8cm)
	10½	8½	40.5	10.22" (26.2cm)	12½	11½	45.5	11.39" (29.2cm)
	11	9	41	10.37" (26.6cm)	13	12	46	11.54" (29.6cm)
	11½	9½	41.5	10.57" (27.1cm)	13½	12½	46.5	11.74" (30.1cm)
	12	10	42	10.73" (27.5cm)	14	13	47	11.97" (30.7cm)

Tips and Tricks for Custom Fitting

Width

If your calf is very shapely, or is outside that average range, you may need to make a few adjustments for a perfect fit. One option is to add additional width by going up a needle size at the point in the pattern where you need more room, and then go back to the original needle further down the leg.

Length

To add up to 3" (7.5cm) to the length of a knee-high without changing the shaping section, add half of the extra length to the top (either in the ribbing or in the rounds worked before shaping) and the other half to the bottom (the rounds worked after final shaping and the top of the heel flap).

To add more than 3" (7.5cm) to the length of a knee-high, work an additional round or two between shaping rounds.

Depending on the pattern, adjustments for subtracting length can be made for up to 2" (5cm) by subtracting half of the length change from the top (either in the ribbing or in the rounds worked before shaping) and half from the bottom (the rounds worked after final shaping and the top of the heel flap).

To shorten the leg by more than 2" (5cm), subtract one round from the rounds between shaping rounds.

Negative Ease

A garment has negative ease when the measured circumference of the garment is less than the measurement of your body. For socks and knee-highs knit in Stockinette stitch, I recommend approximately a 10% difference. For patterns featuring ribs and lace, raise this to a 10–12% difference. For colorwork patterns or heavier yarns, try a 5% difference as there is less stretch in these patterns. And don't forget you are wearing the inside measurement, not the outside.

Making Knee-Highs Stay Up

Go down one or more needle sizes to work the ribbing at the top of the knee-high.

If you have a shapely leg, cast on 10% fewer stitches for the ribbing and use a smaller needle.

Knit a hem, fold it over, and insert ½"-wide (1.5cm) lingerie elastic. (Be sure to use lingerie elastic rather than regular elastic. It will make the top fit snugly but will not cut off the circulation, thereby not leaving the wearer with blue feet!)

Work the middle 1/3 of the ribbing in garter stitch.

Knit a garter, tie it around the ribbing (or knit a row of eyelets and thread it through these). Make the ribbing long enough to be folded over the garter.

Garter Pattern

This quick pattern is done in garter stitch. (Garter stitch is so-called for just this reason—it makes the perfect garter!)

Multiply the number of stitches per inch called for in your pattern by 2¼. Using the needle called for in the main part of the pattern, work as follows:

Row 1: Slip the first stitch purlwise, knit across.

Repeat Row 1 until the Garter measures approximately 30" (76cm), and bind off all stitches.

Avoiding Folds at the Ankle

If your socks normally sit with a wrinkle or fold at the point where the ankle becomes the foot, knit a shorter heel flap.

If you find socks seem tight through the instep and tend to pull, knit a slightly longer heel flap.

Projects

The designs in this book have been inspired by traditional patterns and stitches from around the world. I grew up in an ethnically diverse neighborhood near Winnipeg, Manitoba, in Canada, and my own background is very diverse as well. Many of the women surrounding me during my childhood were knitters, and they had their favorite versions of stitches and patterns. They were more than willing to help me master them when I was still a small girl. Some of these stitches can be found in well-known stitch books by different names; for example, I have seen the lace stitch used in *Czarina's Lace Knee-Highs* on page 70 called Oriel Stitch. However, the name used here honors the lady who showed me how to do a yarn over, and has the title she used.

For your first pair of knee-highs try one of the rib patterns. *Counterpane Knee-Highs* on page 98 are an excellent choice for a first pair, as are *Stalking Stockings* on page 102. Lace patterns are more forgiving for fit as well—keep this in mind if you are knitting for a gift.

One aim of this book, and the projects, is to encourage you to make each pattern your own. The patterns give full instructions for a knee-high and one (or more) alternate sock style. Directions are given on pages 16–17 for converting the knee-high patterns to socks, short socks with turnback cuffs or fitted legwarmers. Have fun with the patterns! You have an official license to change things.

If you need inspiration for your own changes, the knitters who helped me knit these socks were encouraged to express themselves a little. The *Celeigh Knee-Highs* on page 44, for example, were to be knit in two shades of green; however, one was done in olive and green while the other was done in green and cream. Although they are different, they can easily be worn together. The *Celeigh Sock* on page 49 is done exactly as the pattern calls for, except that the knitter moved everything over one block, resulting in her own unique take on the pattern. On the *Flora Knee-Highs* on page 58 we went a little wild and crazy with the colors for the knee-highs while the socks are more subtle. The knitter put her stamp on these by knitting rows of stripes before the toe shaping so the flower wouldn't be cut in half. Let your imagination go and knit the knee-highs of your dreams!

Bonnie Birds Knee-Highs

The inspiration for these came from a picture my Ukrainian grandmother embroidered for me when I was a child. Birds like these were very popular in needlepoint and cross stitch in the latter half of the 19th and first half of the 20th century.

The shaping for this pair is done down each side with leaves and vines. The "ribbon" at the top of the sock is an easy slip stitch pattern my Shetland great-grandmother used when she wanted to dress up a garment.

SIZE

Small/Medium (Large, Extra Large)

FINISHED MEASUREMENTS

To fit foot up to an 8" (8½", 9") (20.5cm [21.5cm, 23cm]) circumference

YARN

1 (3½oz./100g, 400yd./366m) skein solid fingering weight yarn (MC)

1 (4oz./113g, 400yd./366m) skein variegated fingering weight yarn (CC)

The knee-highs shown here were made using Sheila's Sock Yarn (merino wool/nylon, 3½oz./100g, 400yd./366m) in color Cream (MC) and Black Bunny Fibers Superwash Merino Classic (100% superwash merino wool, 4oz./113g, 400yd./366m) in color Delft Blue (CC).

NEEDLES

Set of 5 US 3 (3mm) dpns or 2 circular needles, or size needed to obtain gauge

Set of 5 dpns or 2 circular needles 1 size smaller

NOTIONS

Stitch markers

Yarn needle

GAUGE

17 sts = 2" (5cm) in patt, after blocking

LEG

With long-tail cast on, MC and smaller needles, CO 90 (94, 100) sts. Join in a rnd, being careful not to twist sts. Work in k1, p1 rib for 10 rnds. Change to larger needles. Knit 1 rnd, inc 0 (1, 0) sts—90 (95, 100) sts. Join CC.

Rnd 1: K2, sl 1 wyib, *k4, sl 1 wyib; rep from * to last 2 sts, k2.

Rnd 2: P2, sl 1 wyib, *p4, sl 1 wyib; rep from * to last 2 sts, p2.

Rnds 3–6: Rep Rnds 1–2.

Rnd 7: Rep Rnd 1. Break off CC.

Rnd 8: With MC, dec 0 (1, 0) sts—90 (94, 100) sts. Change to smaller needles and work 10 rnds of k1, p1 rib. Change to larger needles and knit 1 rnd with MC, inc 4 (4, 2) sts evenly around—94 (98, 102) sts. Follow Chart 1 (page 22), beg with Rnd 1, until piece measures approx 13" (33cm)—66 (70, 74) sts. For a longer sock, continue to knit following the Instep Chart (page 23) until you are ready to begin the Heel Flap.

HEEL FLAP

Move the last 2 (3, 3) sts to beg of rnd. Place these sts, plus the first 30 (31, 33) sts of rnd on needle for Heel Flap—32 (34, 36) Heel sts. Place rem 34 (36, 38) sts on hold for Instep.

Row 1 (RS): With CC, knit across Heel sts (slide work back to beg of needle).

Row 2 (RS): With MC, *sl 1, k1; rep from * across (both yarns are now at same end of needle).

Row 3 (WS): With CC, purl across (slide work back to beg of needle).

Row 4 (WS): With MC, *p1, sl 1; rep from * across (both yarns are now at same end of needle).

Rep Rows 1–4 a total of 6 (7, 7) times, then work Rows 1–2 again 1 (0, 1) time more for a total of 26 (28, 30) rows. Break off CC.

TURN HEEL

Work in MC only.

Row 1 (RS): K16 (18, 19), ssk, k1, turn.

Row 2: Sl 1, p1 (3, 3), p2tog, p1, turn.

Row 3: Sl 1, k2 (4, 4), ssk, k1, turn.

Row 4: Sl 1, p3 (5, 5), p2tog, p1, turn. Cont in this manner until all sts have been worked, ending with a WS row—16 (18, 20) sts. Break yarn.

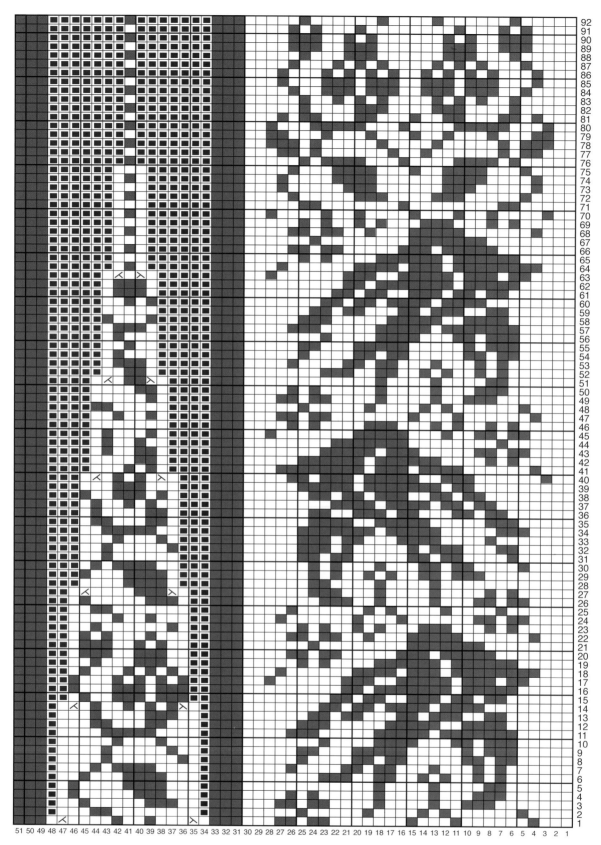

Chart 1

Knit all stitches for size extra large only. For size large, omit stitches 32 and 50. For size small/medium, omit stitches 1, 30, 32 and 50.

GUSSET

With MC, pick up and knit 14 (15, 16) sts along side of Heel Flap, knit across Heel sts, pick up and knit 14 (15, 16) sts along opposite side of Heel Flap. AT THE SAME TIME, place markers on Heel to mark center 34 (36, 38) sts. Beg rnd with Instep sts—78 (84, 90) sts.

Rnd 1: Work Instep Chart across 34 (36, 38) Instep sts, maintaining patt. On Heel sts, work *with MC, k1; with CC, k1; rep from * to marker, with MC, k2 (0, 1), knit Heel Chart across next 30 (36, 36) sts, with MC, k2 (0, 1), **with CC, k1; with MC, k1; rep from ** to end of rnd.

Rnd 2: Work Instep as established. On Heel sts, with MC, ssk, work in stripe patt as established to marker, with MC, k2 (0, 1), work in patt across 30 (36, 36) sts, with MC, k2 (0, 1), work in stripe patt to end.

Rep Rnds 1–2 until 34 (36, 38) sts rem on Heel—68 (72, 76) sts. Final dec will be worked on st before and after each marker, with MC. Work even in patt until piece measures approx 2½" (6.5cm) less than desired length.

TOE

Rnd 1: With MC, *sl 1, k1; rep from * around.

Rnd 2: *With CC, k1, ssk, knit to last 3 sts, k2tog, k1; rep from * across Heel sts.

Rep Rnds 1–2 maintaining the established dot patt until 16 sts rem.

FINISHING

Graft Toe using Kitchener stitch. Weave in ends.

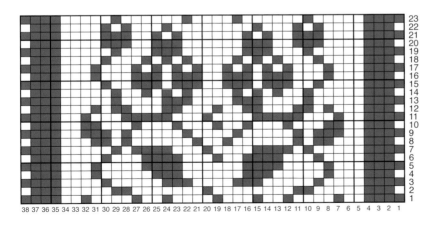

Instep Chart

Knit all stitches for size extra large. For size large, omit stitches 3 and 36. For size small/medium, omit stitches 3, 5, 34 and 36.

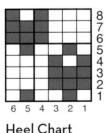

Heel Chart

Bonnie Birds Socks

LEG

Using long-tail cast on, MC and smaller needles, CO 66 (70, 74) sts.

Join in a rnd, being careful not to twist sts. Work in k1, p1 rib for 10 rnds. Change to larger needles. Knit 1 rnd, dec 1 (0, 0) st and inc 0 (0, 1) sts—65 (70, 75) sts. Join CC.

Rnd 1: K2, sl 1 wyib, *k4, sl 1 wyib; rep from * to last 2 sts, k2.

Rnd 2: P2, sl 1 wyib, *p4, sl 1 wyib; rep from * to last 2 sts, p2.

Rnds 3–6: Rep Rnds 1–2.

Rnd 7: Rep Rnd 1. Break off CC.

Rnd 8: With MC, inc 1 (0, 0) st and dec 0 (0, 1) sts—66 (70, 74) sts. Change to smaller needles and work 10 rnds of k1, p1 rib. Change to larger needles and knit 1 rnd with MC. Follow Sock Chart, beg with Rnd 1, until piece measures approx 8" (20.5cm)—66 (70, 74) sts. For a longer sock, continue to knit following the Instep Chart (page 23) until you are ready to begin the Heel Flap. Finish Sock as for Knee-High from Heel Flap to Finishing.

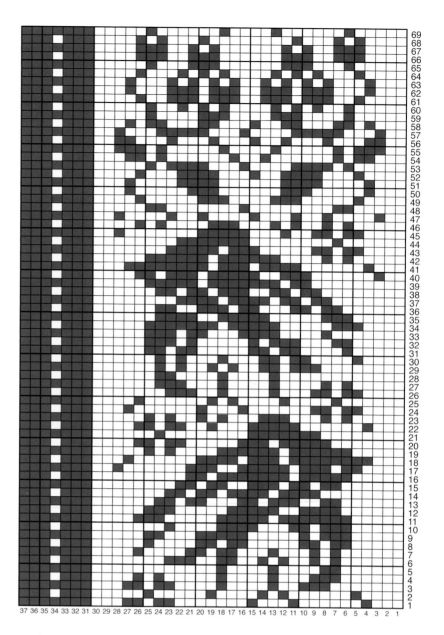

Sock Chart

Knit all stitches for size extra large only. For size large, omit stitches 1 and 30. For size small/medium, omit stitches 1, 30, 32 and 36.

The sock shown here was made using Dragonfly Fibers Dragon Sock Yarn (100% superwash merino wool, 4oz./113g, 400yd./366m) in color Beachgrass (MC) and Yarn Love Sock (60% Superfine Merino/20% Bamboo/15% Silk, 1³/₄oz./50g, 195yd./178m) in color Blackberry Jam (CC).

Birdwalk Knee-Highs

This pattern draws design inspiration from diverse places: a 19th century embroidery magazine in a museum in Iceland, and a Thunderbird motif from an antique Cowichan basket. The shaping is done down both sides of the leg.

SIZE

Small/Medium (Large, Extra Large)

FINISHED MEASUREMENTS

To fit foot up to an 8" (8½", 9") (20.5cm [21.5cm, 23cm]) circumference

YARN

2 (4oz./113g, 400yd./366m) skeins fingering weight yarn; 1 skein each of 2 colors (MC and CC)

The knee-highs shown here were made using Black Bunny Fibers Superwash Merino Classic (100% superwash merino wool, 4oz./113g, 400yd./366m) in colors Anthracite (MC) and Pewter (CC).

NEEDLES

Set of 5 US 3 (3mm) dpns or 2 circular needles, or size needed to obtain gauge

Set of 5 dpns or 2 circular needles 1 size smaller

NOTIONS

Stitch markers

Yarn needle

GAUGE

18 sts = 2" (5cm) in patt, after blocking

LEG

Using long-tail cast on, smaller needles and CC, CO 93 (96, 99) sts. Join in a rnd, being careful not to twist sts. Work in k2, p1 rib for 2" (5cm). Change to larger needles and with CC, knit 1 rnd, inc 3 (4, 5) sts evenly around—96 (100, 104) sts.

Rnd 1: *With MC, k1; with CC, k1; rep from * around.

Rnd 2: *With CC, k1; with MC, k1; rep from * around.

Rep Rnds 1–2 a total of 2 times, then rep Rnd 1 once more. With MC, knit 1 rnd, placing markers after the first 17 (17, 19) sts, after the next 31 (33, 33) sts, and after the next 17 (17, 19) sts—96 (100, 104) sts. Shaping is worked in the 17- (17-, 19-) st sections.

Rnd 1: **With CC, k2; *with MC, k1; with CC, k1; rep from * to 2 sts before marker, with CC, k2; work Pattern Chart across next 31 (33, 33) sts; rep from ** once more to complete rnd.

Rnd 2: **With CC, k2; *with CC, k1; with MC, k1; rep from * to 2 sts before marker, with CC, k2; work Pattern Chart as before; rep from ** once more to complete rnd.

Rep Rnds 1–2, and, AT THE SAME TIME, on every 12th rnd work shaping as follows until 72 (76, 80) sts rem:

On shaping sections only, with CC, k1, ssk; work in patt to 3 sts before marker, with CC, k2tog, k1. Work in established patt until piece measures 13" (33cm).

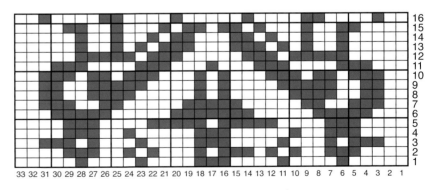

Pattern Chart

Knit stitches 1–33 for sizes large and extra large. For size small/medium, knit stitches 2–32 only.

Heel Flap

Move first 2 (2, 4) sts of rnd to end. Place next 37 (39, 41) sts on needle for Heel Flap. Rem 35 (37, 39) sts are placed on hold for Instep. Break yarn.

With RS facing, join CC and knit across Heel sts, inc 1 (1,1) st—38 (40, 42) sts.

Slide work back to beg of needle, and with MC, knit across.

Both yarns are now at same end of needle.

Row 1 (WS): With CC, *sl 1, p1; rep from * across.

Row 2 (WS): Slide work back to beg of needle. With MC, purl across. Both yarns are now at same end of needle.

Row 3 (RS): With CC, *sl 1, k1; rep from * across.

Row 4 (RS): Slide work back to beg of needle. With MC, knit across. Both yarns are now at same end of needle.

Rep Rows 1–4 a total of 6 (7, 7) times, then work Rows 1–2 again 1 (0, 1) time more for a total of 26 (28, 30) rows. Break off CC.

Turn Heel

Work in MC only.

Row 1 (RS): K19 (20, 21), ssk, k1, turn.

Row 2: Sl 1, p1, p2tog, p1, turn.

Row 3: Sl 1, k2, ssk, k1, turn.

Cont in this manner, working 1 more st before dec each time until all sts have been worked, ending with a purl row—20 (20, 22) sts. Break yarn.

Gusset

With MC, pick up and knit 14 (15, 16) sts down Heel Flap. Knit across Heel sts. Pick up and knit 14 (15, 16) sts along opposite side of Heel Flap. Work Instep Chart across Instep sts—83 (87, 93) sts, 48 (50, 54) Heel sts.

Rnd 1: *With MC, k1; with CC, k1; rep from * across Heel sts, work Instep sts in patt.

Rnd 2: *With CC, k1, with MC, k1; rep from * across Heel sts, work Instep sts in patt.

Rnd 3: With CC, ssk, work as for Rnd 1 across Heel sts to last 2 sts, with CC, k2tog, work Instep sts in patt. Rep Rnds 2–3 until 36 (38, 40) Heel sts rem. Work even in dot patt until piece measures 1½" (4cm) less than desired length.

Toe

With CC, knit 1 rnd.

Rnd 1: Work in MC. Across Heel sts, work k1, ssk, *sl 1, k1; rep from * to last 3 sts, k2tog, k1; across Instep, work k1, ssk, *sl 1, k1; rep from * to last 4 sts, sl 1, k2tog, k1.

Rnd 2: With CC, knit.

Rep Rnds 1–2 until 27 (27, 31) sts rem, ending with Rnd 1. With CC, knit 1 rnd, dec 1 st on Heel—26 (26, 30) sts.

Finishing

Graft Toe using Kitchener stitch. Weave in ends.

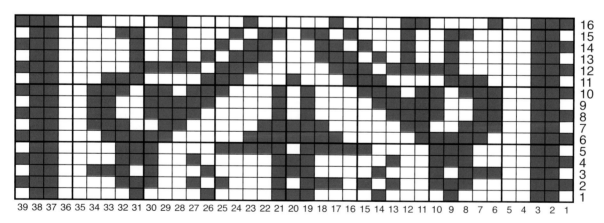

Instep Chart

Knit all stitches for size extra large only. For size large, omit stitches 1 and 39.

For size small/medium, omit stitches 1, 4, 36 and 39.

Birdwalk Legwarmers

Making these legwarmers is as simple as making the knee-highs without the foot. Please note the changes in sizing, measurements and yarn below.

SIZE

Small/Medium (Large, Extra Large)

FINISHED MEASUREMENTS

To fit ankle up to an 8" (8½", 9") (20.5cm [21.5cm, 23cm]) circumference

YARN

2 (3½oz./100g, 437yd./400m) skeins fingering weight yarn; 1 skein each of 2 colors (MC and CC)

LEG

Using long-tail cast on, smaller needles and CC, CO 93 (96, 99) sts. Join in a rnd, being careful not to twist sts. Work in k2, p1 rib for 2" (5cm). Change to larger needles and with CC, knit 1 rnd, inc 3 (4, 5) sts evenly around—96 (100, 104) sts.

Rnd 1: *With MC, k1; with CC, k1; rep from * around.

Rnd 2: *With CC, k1; with MC, k1; rep from * around.

Rep Rnds 1–2 a total of 2 times, then rep Rnd 1 once more. With MC, knit 1 rnd, placing markers after the first 17 (17, 19) sts, after the next 31 (33, 33) sts, and after the next 17 (17, 19) sts—96 (100, 104) sts. Shaping is worked in the 17- (17-, 19-) st sections.

Rnd 1: **With CC, k2; *with MC, k1; with CC, k1; rep from * to 2 sts before marker, with CC, k2; work Pattern Chart (page 27) across next 31 (33, 33) sts; rep from ** once more to complete rnd.

Rnd 2: **With CC, k2; *with CC, k1; with MC, k1; rep from * to 2 sts before marker, with CC, k2; work Pattern Chart (page 27) as before; rep from ** once more to complete rnd.

Rep Rnds 1–2, and, AT THE SAME TIME, on every 12th rnd work shaping as follows until 72 (76, 80) sts rem:

On shaping sections only, with CC, k1, ssk; work in patt to 3 sts before marker, with CC, k2tog, k1. Work even in established patt until piece measures 13" (33cm). Break off MC. Change to smaller needles and with CC work in k2, p1 rib for 2" (5cm). Bind off all sts.

The legwarmers shown here were made using Cascade Heritage (75% superwash merino wool/25% nylon, 3½oz./100g, 437yd./400m) in colors #5604 (MC) and #5602 (CC).

Eric's Path Knee-Highs

The design on this pair of knee-highs was adapted from old Icelandic embroidery charts and Celtic carvings. It reminded me of a pathway through an old garden. The shaping is done down each side in a stranded pattern.

SIZE

Small/Medium (Large, Extra Large)

FINISHED MEASUREMENTS

To fit foot up to an 8¼" (8¾", 9¼") (21cm [22cm, 23.5cm]) circumference

YARN

2 (3½oz./100g, 490yd./448m) skeins fingering weight yarn, 1 each of 2 colors (MC and CC)

The knee-highs shown here were made using Gypsy Knits Sock It! (superwash merino, 3½oz./100g, 490yd./448m) in colors Ventura Blvd (MC) and Bourbon Street (CC).

NEEDLES

Set of 5 US 3 (3mm) dpns or 2 circular needles, or size needed to obtain gauge

Set of 5 dpns or 2 circular needles 1 size smaller

NOTIONS

Stitch markers

Yarn needle

GAUGE

17 sts = 2" (5cm) in patt, after blocking

LEG

Using long-tail cast on, smaller needles and CC, CO 93 (96, 99) sts. Join in a rnd, being careful not to twist sts. Work in k2, p1 rib for 10 rnds. Change to larger needles. Knit 1 rnd, inc 3 (0, 3) sts evenly around—96 (96, 102) sts. Work Band Chart. With CC, dec 3 (0, 3) sts—93 (96, 99) sts. Change to smaller needles. Knit in k2, p1 rib for 10 rnds, inc 3 (4, 5) sts on last rnd—96 (100, 104) sts. Change to larger needles and MC. Knit 1 rnd. Beg Chart 1 (page 32). Work until piece measures approx 13" (33cm)—70 (74, 78) sts.

HEEL FLAP

Heel is worked on first 35 (37, 39) sts of rnd. Place rem 35 (37, 39) sts on hold for Instep. With MC, knit, inc 1 st on Heel sts—36 (38, 40) sts.

Set-Up Row (RS): Slide work back to beg of needle. With CC, *sl 1, k1; rep from * across.

Row 1 (WS): Both yarns are now at same end of needle. With MC, sl 1, purl across.

Row 2 (WS): Slide work back to beg of needle. With CC, *p1, sl; rep from * across.

Row 3 (RS): Both yarns are now at same end of needle. With MC, *k1, sl 1; rep from * across.

Row 4 (RS): Slide work back to beg of needle. With CC, sl 1, knit across.

Rep Rows 1–4 8 (9, 10) times more, then work Rows 1–2 once more. Break off CC.

TURN HEEL

Row 1 (RS): K18 (19, 20) ssk, k1, turn.

Row 2: Sl 1, p1, p2tog, p1, turn.

Row 3: Sl 1 pwise, knit to 1 st before gap, ssk, k1, turn.

Row 4: Sl 1 pwise, purl to 1 st before gap, p2tog, p1, turn.

Rep Rows 3–4 until all sts have been worked—18 (19, 20) sts. Break yarn.

Band Chart

Chart 1

In this chart:

- Knit all stitches for size extra large only. For size large, omit stitches 14-15 and 51-52. For size small/medium, omit stitches 14-17 and 49-52.
- The beginning of the second repeat for the knee-high starts at stitch 12 and ends at stitch 54; again, for size large omit stitches 14-15 and 51-52. For size small/medium, omit stitches 14-17 and 49-52.
- Stitch 33 is the center back and front of sock.

GUSSET

Join yarn at end of Instep, and with MC pick up and knit 17 (18, 21) sts along side of Heel Flap, knit across 18 (19, 20) Heel sts, dec 1 (0, 1) st, pick up and knit 17 (18, 21) sts along opposite side of Heel Flap—51 (55, 61) Heel sts. Join CC and work across Instep sts, maintaining patt. Pm 8 (9, 11) sts in from each end of Heel sts.

Rnd 1: On Heel sts *with CC, k1; with MC, k1; rep from * to marker, knit Heel Chart to second marker, rep stripe patt on rem Heel sts, work Instep sts in patt.

Rnds 2 and 4: With CC, ssk; work in patt to last 2 Heel sts, with CC, k2tog; work Instep sts in patt.

Rnd 3: Work even in patt.

Rep Rnds 3–4 until 70 (74, 78) sts rem. Work even until piece measures 2" (5cm) less than desired length. With CC, knit 1 rnd.

TOE

Rnd 1: With MC, *k1, sl 1; rep from * across Heel sts, ending with k1. Rep on Instep sts.

Rnds 2 and 4: With CC, k1, ssk, knit across Heel sts to last 3 sts, k2tog, k1. Rep on Instep sts.

Rnd 3: With MC, k1, *k1, sl 1; rep from * across Heel sts, ending k2. Rep on Instep sts.

Rep Rnds 1–4, maintaining stripe patt, until 22 sts rem.

FINISHING

Graft Toe using Kitchener stitch. Weave in ends.

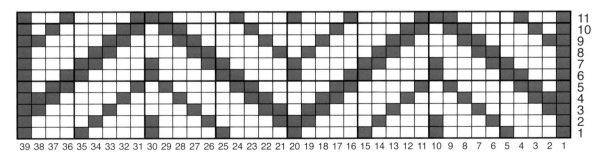

Heel Chart

Knit all stitches for size extra large only. For size large, omit stitches 2 and 38. For size small/medium, omit stitches 2, 3, 37 and 38.

Eric's Path Socks

The colorwork pattern from the knee-highs translates beautifully into a sock. Please note the changes in yarn below.

····················· Y A R N

4 (1³/₄oz./50g, 165yd./150m) skeins fingering weight yarn, 2 each of 2 colors (MC and CC)

LEG

Using long-tail cast on, smaller needles and CC, CO 69 (75, 78) sts. Join in a rnd, being careful not to twist sts. Work in k2, p1 rib for 2" (5cm). On last rnd, inc 1 (0, 0) st and dec 0 (1, 0) sts—70 (74, 78) sts. Change to larger needles. Knit 1 rnd. Beg Sock Pattern Chart. Work until piece measures approx 8" (20.5cm) or desired length. Finish Sock as for Knee-High from Heel Flap to Finishing.

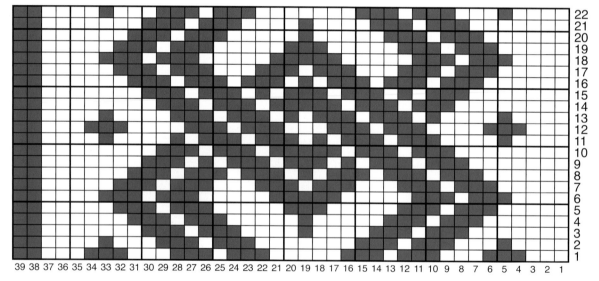

Sock Pattern Chart

Knit all stitches for size extra large only. For size large, omit stitches 2 and 36. For size small/medium, omit stitches 2, 3, 35 and 36.

The socks shown here were made using Sandnessgarn Mini Alpakka (100% pure alpaca, 1³/₄oz./50g, 165yd./150m) in colors 4081 (MC) and 3911 (CC).

Both Sides Now Knee-Highs

Many North Atlantic cultures use positive/negative images or mirror images in their designs. Use your imagination in working this design. Make the knee-highs match or make each one opposite to the other. You could also have the mirror image on one sock, front and back. The shaping in this pattern is done down the sides.

SIZE

Small/Medium (Large, Extra Large)

FINISHED MEASUREMENTS

To fit foot up to an 8" (8³⁄₄", 9¹⁄₂") (20.5cm [22cm, 24cm]) circumference

YARN

2 (3¹⁄₂oz./100g, 490yd./448m) skeins fingering weight yarn, 1 in each of 2 colors (MC and CC)

The knee-highs shown here were made using Gypsy Knits Sock It! (superwash merino, 3¹⁄₂oz./100g, 490yd./448m) in color Pottery (MC) and Socks 2Dye4 (superwash merino, 3¹⁄₂oz./100g, 490yd./448m) in color Cream (CC).

NEEDLES

Set of 5 US 3 (3mm) dpns or 2 circular needles, or size needed to obtain gauge

NOTIONS

Stitch markers
Yarn needle

GAUGE

17 sts = 2" (5cm) in patt, after blocking

LEG

Using long-tail cast on and CC, CO 92 (96, 104) sts. Join in a rnd, being careful not to twist sts. Work in k2, p2 rib for 1³⁄₄" (4.5cm). Knit 1 rnd, inc 0 (2, 2) sts—92 (98, 106) sts.

Next rnd: *K33 (36, 40), pm, k13 (shaping area), pm; rep from * once more. Proceed as follows:

Option 1: Knit 1 knee-high using Chart 1A, other knee-high using Chart 1B.

Option 2: Work first patt section of each knee-high using Chart 1A, and second using Chart 1B. Select Shaping Chart 1 or 2 (page 38) as desired to contrast or coordinate with colorwork.

Work Chart 1A or 1B over each 33- (36-, 40-) st section and Shaping Chart 1 or 2 over each 13-st shaping area. Work until piece measures 13" (33cm)—68 (74, 82) sts.

HEEL FLAP

Place with first 33 (36, 40) sts of rnd on 1 needle for Heel. Place rem 35 (38, 42) sts on hold for Instep.

Set-Up Row (RS): With CC, knit, dec 0 (1, 1) sts—33 (35, 39) sts.

Row 1 (RS): Slide work back to beg of needle. With MC, *sl 1, k1; rep from * to last st, sl 1.

Row 2 (WS): Both yarns now at same end of needle. With CC, purl across.

Row 3 (WS): Slide work back to beg of needle. With MC, *sl 1, p1; rep from * to last st, sl 1.

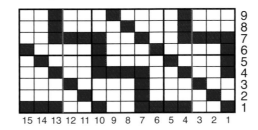

Chart 1A

For size small/medium, knit sts 1–3, then rep sts 4–12 until 3 sts remain, then knit sts 13–15. For size large, rep only sts 4–12. For size extra large, knit sts 2–3, then rep sts 4–12 until 2 sts rem, then knit sts 13–14.

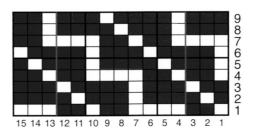

Chart 1B

For size small/medium, knit sts 1–3, then rep sts 4–12 until 3 sts remain, then knit sts 13–15. For size large, rep only sts 4–12. For size extra large, knit sts 2–3, then rep sts 4–12 until 2 sts rem, then knit sts 13–14.

Row 4 (RS): Both yarns are now at same end of needle. With CC, knit across.

Rep Rows 1–4 a total of 15 (16, 17) times. Break off MC. With CC, purl, inc 1 (1, 1) st—34 (36, 40) Heel sts.

TURN HEEL

Row 1 (RS): K18 (19, 21), ssk, k1, turn.

Row 2: Sl 1, p3, p2tog, p1, turn.

Row 3: Sl 1, k4, ssk, k1, turn.

Row 4: Sl 1, p5, p2tog, p1, turn.

Cont in this manner, working 1 more st before dec each row until all sts have been worked—18 (20, 22) sts. Break yarn.

GUSSET

Join CC. Pick up and knit 16 (17, 18) sts along side of Heel Flap, knit across 18 (20, 22) Heel sts, inc 1 st, pick up and knit 16 (17, 18) sts along opposite side of Heel Flap—51 (55, 59) Heel sts. Pm 8 (9, 10) sts in from each end of Heel sts.

Rnds 1 and 2: Work 35 (38, 42) Instep sts in patt, across Heel sts *with CC, k1; with MC, k1; rep from * to marker, ending with MC (CC, MC), work Heel Chart to marker, work in alternating color patt as before, beg with MC (CC, MC) and ending with CC, k1.

Rnd 3: Work as for Rnd 1 across Instep, with CC, ssk; work stripes as established to marker, work Heel Chart to next marker, work stripes to last 2 sts, with CC, k2tog.

Rep Rnds 2–3 until 35 (37, 39) Heel sts rem. Work even in patt until piece measures 2" (5cm) less than desired length.

TOE

Rnd 1: With CC, knit, dec 0 (1, 3) sts on Instep—35 (37, 39) sts, 70 (74, 78) sts total.

Rnd 2: K1, ssk, knit to last 3 Instep sts, k2tog, k1; rep across Heel.

Rep Rnds 1–2 until 38 (38, 40) sts rem. Rep Rnd 2 only until 22 (22, 24) sts rem. Size extra large only: Work Rnd 2 dec on Instep sts only on last dec rnd.

FINISHING

Graft Toe using Kitchener stitch. Weave in ends.

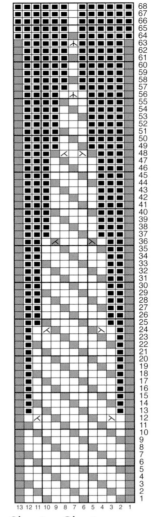

Shaping Chart 1

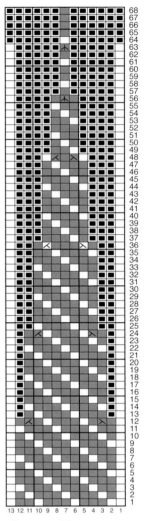

Shaping Chart 2

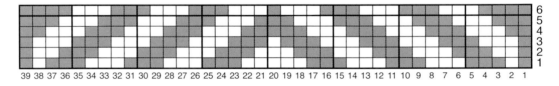

Heel Chart

Knit all stitches for size extra large only. For size large, omit stitches 2 and 38. For size small/medium, omit stitches 2, 3, 37 and 38.

38

Both Sides Now Socks and Anklets

This sock features different yarn requirements than the knee-high. To create the ankle socks pictured, use the instructions on page 16 for converting a knee-high pattern to a short sock with a turnback cuff.

YARN

2 (3½oz./100g, 430yd./393m) skeins fingering weight yarn, 1 each of 2 colors (MC and CC)

LEG

With CC, CO 68 (72, 80) sts. Join in a rnd, being careful not to twist sts. Work in k2, p2 rib for 1¾" (4.5cm). Knit 1 rnd, inc 0 (2, 2) sts—68 (74, 82) sts.

Next rnd: *K33 (36, 40), pm, k1, pm; rep from * once more. Proceed as follows:

Option 1: Knit 1 sock using Chart 1A (page 37), the other sock using Chart 1B (page 37).

Option 2: Work the first patt section of each sock using Chart 1A, and the second using Chart 1B.

Work Chart 1A or 1B over each 33- (36-, 40-) st section and with CC, k1 over each 1-st section. Work until piece measures 6" (15cm) or desired length. Finish Sock as for Knee-High from Heel Flap to Finishing.

The sock shown here was made using Three Irish Girls Adorn Sock (80% merino wool/20% nylon, 3½oz./100g, 430yd./393m) in colors Ginger Honey (MC) and Serenity (CC). The anklet shown here was made using Schoolhouse Press Satakieli (100% wool, 1¾oz./50g, 180yd./165m) in colors #003 Cream (MC) and #385 Brown (CC).

Katya's Fancy Knee-Highs

This pattern is adapted from mittens my neighbor knitted for me when I was a child. She came to Canada from Siberia in the late 1940s and brought her patterns with her in her mind and in her fingers. We called her Mrs. Katya.

The shaping for this pair of knee-highs is done down each side. The sizing goes up to a large width, as these would be very suitable for a man.

SIZE

Small/Medium (Large, Extra Large)

FINISHED MEASUREMENTS

To fit foot up to an 8¾" (9¼", 10") (22cm [23.5cm, 25.5cm]) circumference

YARN

3 (1¾oz./50g, 202yd./185m) skeins fingering weight yarn, 2 skeins MC and 1 skein CC

The knee-highs shown here were made using Filandia Fata (superwash wool, 1¾oz./50g, 202yd./185m) in colors #82 Light Gray (MC) and #22 Dark Blue (CC).

NEEDLES

Set of 5 US 3 (3mm) dpns or 2 circular needles, or size needed to obtain gauge

Set of 5 dpns or 2 circular needles 1 size smaller

NOTIONS

Stitch markers

Yarn needle

GAUGE

16 sts = 2" (5cm) in patt, after blocking

LEG

Using long-tail cast on, smaller needles and CC, CO 98 (106, 114) sts. Join in a rnd, being careful not to twist the sts. With MC, work in k1, p1 rib for 1½" (4cm). On last rnd, pm for shaping areas as follows: Work 36 (40, 44) sts in rib patt, pm, work next 13 sts in rib patt (shaping area), pm, work 36 (40, 44) sts in rib patt, pm, work next 13 sts in rib patt (shaping area). Change to larger needles. Knit 1 rnd.

Next rnd: *Work Rnd 1 of appropriate Chart 1 for your size over 36 (40, 44) sts, work Shaping Chart over next 13 sts; rep from * once more. Cont as established until piece measures 13" (33cm)—72 (80, 88) sts.

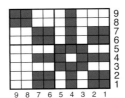

Chart 1—Size Small/Medium

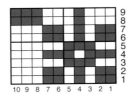

Chart 1—Size Large

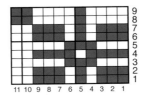

Chart 1—Size Extra Large

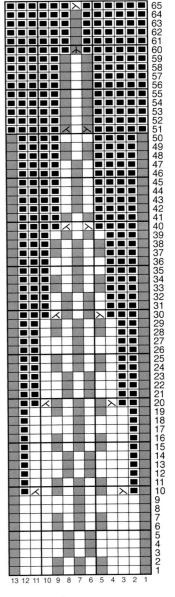

Shaping Chart

41

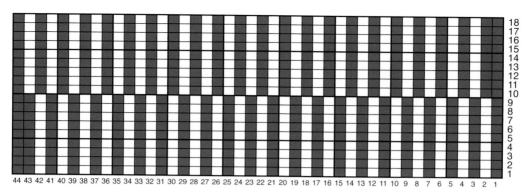

Heel Chart

Knit all stitches for size extra large only. For size large, omit stitches 2–3 and 42–43. For size small/medium, omit stitches 2–5 and 40–43.

HEEL FLAP

Move last st to beg of rnd. Work first 36 (40, 44) sts for Heel Flap. Place rem 36 (40, 44) sts on hold for Instep. With CC, knit 1 row, purl 1 row across Heel sts.

Row 1 (RS): *Sl 1, k1; rep from * across.

Row 2: Sl 1, purl to end.

Rep Rnds 1–2 a total of 15 (17, 19) times.

TURN HEEL

Row 1 (RS): K19 (21, 23), ssk, k1, turn.

Row 2: Sl 1, p3, p2tog, p1, turn.

Row 3: Sl 1, k4, ssk, k1, turn.

Row 4: Sl 1, p5, p2tog, p1, turn.

Cont in this manner, working 1 more st before dec each row until all sts have been worked—20 (22, 24) sts. Break yarn.

GUSSET

With CC, pick up and knit 15 (17, 19) sts along side of Heel Flap, knit across Heel sts, pick up and knit 15 (17, 19) sts along opposite side of Heel Flap, work across Instep sts in patt, dec 0 (1, 0) sts at end of Instep—86 (95, 106) sts. Pm 7 (8, 9) sts in from each end of 50 (56, 62) Heel sts.

Rnd 1: Across Heel sts work *with MC, k1; with CC, k1; rep from * to marker, knit Heel Chart to marker, **with MC, k1; with CC, k1; rep from ** to end; work Instep sts in patt.

Rnd 2: Across Heel sts work with CC, ssk; work in patt to last 2 sts, with CC, k2tog; work Instep sts in patt.

Rep Rnds 1–2 until 70 (73, 78) sts rem. Rep Rnd 1 until piece measures 2" (5cm) less than desired length. With CC, knit 1 rnd.

TOE

Rnd 1: With MC, *k1, sl 1 pwise; rep from * across Heel sts, ending k1; rep across Instep sts.

Rnds 2 and 4: With CC, *k1, ssk, knit to last 3 Heel sts, k2tog, k1; rep across Instep sts.

Rnd 3: With MC, k1, *k1, sl 1 pwise; rep from * across Heel sts, ending k2; rep across Instep sts.

Rep Rnds 1–4, maintaining stripe patt until 24 (23, 24) sts rem.

Next Rnd (size large only): Knit to last 2 sts of Instep, k2tog—22 sts.

FINISHING

Graft Toe using Kitchener stitch. Weave in ends.

Katya's Fancy Anklets

This anklet with turnback cuff features just enough colorwork to add interest to a simple ribbed sock.

YARN

2 (1³⁄₄oz./50g, 202yd./185m) skeins fingering weight yarn, 1 each of 2 colors (MC and CC)

LEG

Using long-tail cast on, smaller needles and CC, CO 72 (80, 88) sts. Join in a rnd, being careful not to twist the sts. With MC, work in k1, p1 rib for ½" (1.5cm). Change to larger needles. Knit 1 rnd. Work all rnds of appropriate Chart 1 for your size (page 41) twice. Knit 1 rnd, purl 1 rnd. Turn work inside out for Cuff turnback. Change to smaller needles. Work in k1, p1 rib or rib of your choice until rib is ½" (1.3cm) longer than turnback cuff. Finish Anklet as for Knee-High from Heel Flap to Finishing, working in Stockinette stitch over Heel sts and in rib patt over Instep sts and Toe.

The sock shown here was made using Filandia Fata (superwash wool, 1³⁄₄oz./50g, 202yd./185m) in colors #82 Light Gray (MC) and #39 Red (CC).

Celeigh Knee-Highs

Whether you call them shamrocks or clovers, these leaves seemed like the right thing to wear to a celeigh—a traditional Gaelic gathering with singing and dancing. The positive/negative element in this design leaves room to experiment with color, and I've done so here by making knee-highs of two different colors. Have fun putting your own stamp on this pair, which features shaping within each pattern stripe.

SIZE

Small/Medium (Large, Extra Large)

FINISHED MEASUREMENTS

To fit foot up to an 8" (8³/₄", 9¹/₂") (20.5cm [22cm, 24cm]) circumference

YARN

3 (1³/₄oz./50g, 246yd./225m) skeins fingering weight yarn, 1 each of 3 colors (MC, CC1 and CC2)

The knee-highs shown here were made using Filandia Boogie Woogie (70% wool/30% acrylic, 1³/₄oz./50g, 246yd./225m) in colors #91 (MC), #99 (CC1) and #11 (CC2).

NEEDLES

Set of 5 US 3 (3mm) dpns or 2 circular needles, or size needed to obtain gauge

Set of 5 dpns or 2 circular needles 1 size smaller

NOTIONS

Stitch markers

Yarn needle

GAUGE

18 sts = 2" (5cm) in patt, after blocking

LEG

Using long-tail cast on, smaller needles and MC, CO 93 (99, 105) sts. Join in a rnd, being careful not to twist sts. Work in k2, p1 rib for 1¹/₂" (4cm). Change to larger needles. Knit 1 rnd, inc 3 (3, 3) sts evenly around—96 (102, 108) sts. Follow appropriate Pattern Chart for your size (pages 47–48) until piece measures 13" (33cm); rep Rnds 61–72 to work even once shaping is complete—72 (78, 84) sts.

HEEL FLAP

First 36 (39, 42) sts are for Heel Flap. Place rem 36 (39, 42) sts on hold for Instep.

Set-Up Row (RS): With MC, knit, dec 1 (0, 1) st—35 (39, 41) sts.

Row 1 (RS): Slide work back to beg of needle. With CC, *k1, sl 1; rep from * to last st, k1.

Row 2 (WS): Both yarns are now at same end of needle. With MC, purl.

Row 3 (WS): Slide work back to beg of needle. With CC, *p1, sl 1; rep from * to last st, p1.

Row 4 (RS): Both yarns are now at same end of needle. With MC, knit.

Rep Rows 1–4 a total of 6 (6, 6) times, then Rows 1–3 once more. Break off CC.

TURN HEEL

Use MC.

Row 1 (RS): K19 (21, 22), ssk, k1, turn.

Row 2: Sl 1, p4, p2tog, p1, turn.

Row 3: Sl 1, k5, ssk, k1, turn.

Row 4: Sl 1, p6, p2tog, p1, turn.

Cont in this manner until all sts have been worked—19 (21, 23) sts. Break yarn.

GUSSET

With MC, pick up and knit 14 (15, 16) sts along side of Heel Flap. Knit across Heel sts. Pick up and knit 14 (15, 16) sts along opposite side of Heel Flap—47 (51, 55) Heel sts. Work the Instep chart for your size, working patt as established.

Pm 5 (6, 7) sts from each end of Heel sts.

Rnd 1: *With MC, k1; with CC, k1; rep from * to marker, work Heel Chart to marker, **with MC, k1; with CC, k1; rep from ** to end of Heel sts; work Instep Chart as established.

Rnd 2: *With CC, k1; with MC, k1; rep from * to marker, work Heel Chart to marker, **with CC, k1; with MC, k1; rep from ** to end of Heel sts; work Instep Chart as established.

Rnd 3: With MC, ssk, work in patt as for Rnd 1 to last 2 sts of Heel, with MC, k2tog; work Instep Chart as established.

Rep Rnds 2–3 until 37 (39, 41) Heel sts rem. Work even until piece measures 1½" (4cm) less than desired length.

TOE

Work 1 rnd in MC, dec 1 (0, 0) st on Heel and dec 0 (0, 1) sts in Instep—72 (78, 82) sts.

Rnd 1: With CC, *k1, sl 1; rep from * across Heel sts, ending with k1. Rep across Instep.

Rnds 2 and 4: With MC, k1, ssk, knit across Heel to last 3 sts, k2tog, k1. Rep across Instep.

Rnd 3: With CC, k1, *k1, sl 1; rep from * across Heel, ending with k2. Rep across Instep.

Rep Rnds 1–4, maintaining patt, until 20 (22, 22) sts rem, ending with Rnd 2.

FINISHING

Graft Toe using Kitchener stitch. Weave in ends.

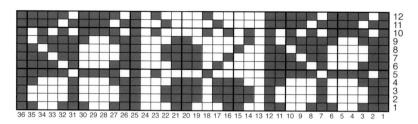

Small/Medium Instep Chart

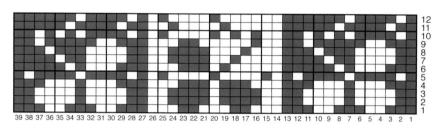

Large Instep Chart

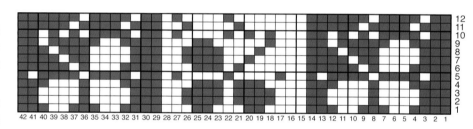

Extra Large Instep Chart

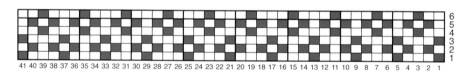

Heel Chart

Knit all stitches for size extra large only. For size large, omit stitches 1 and 41. For size small/medium, omit stitches 1, 2, 40 and 41.

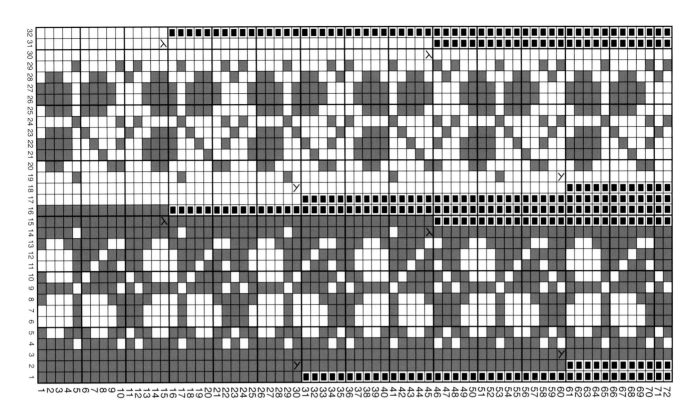

Small/Medium Pattern Chart (chart has been rotated to fit page)

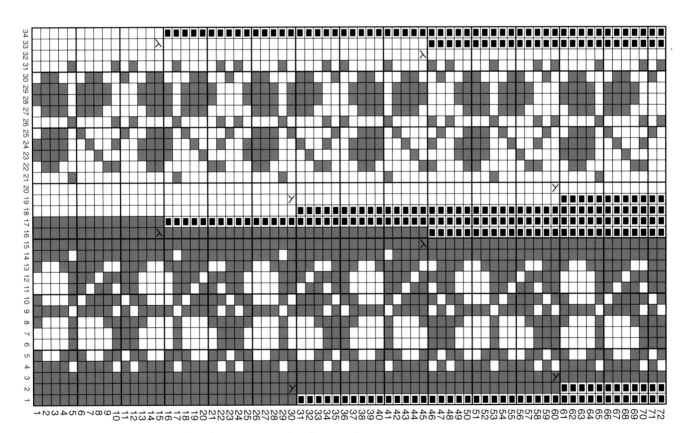

Large Pattern Chart (chart has been rotated to fit page)

47

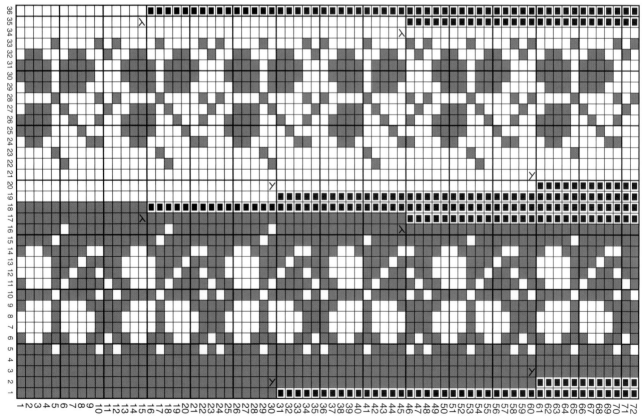

Extra Large Pattern Chart (chart has been rotated to fit page)

Celeigh Socks

These socks are sure to keep your toes tapping at a celeigh, too (even if the toe on the sock isn't as fancy as the toe on the knee-high).

YARN

2 (1³/₄oz./50g, 246yd./225m) skeins fingering weight yarn, 1 each of 2 colors (MC and CC)

LEG

Using long-tail cast on, smaller needles and CC, CO 69 (75, 81) sts. Join in a rnd, being careful not to twist sts. Work in k2, p1 rib for 1¹/₂" (4cm). Change to larger needles. Knit 1 rnd, inc 3 sts evenly around—72 (78, 84) sts. Follow appropriate Sock Pattern Chart for your size until piece measures 8" (20.5cm) or desired length. Finish Sock as for Knee-High from Heel Flap to Finishing, working toe in CC.

The sock shown here was made using Filandia Boogie Woogie (70% wool/30% acrylic, 1³/₄oz./50g, 246yd./225m) in colors #11 (MC) and #99 (CC).

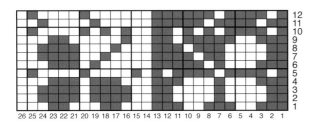

Small/Medium Sock Pattern Chart

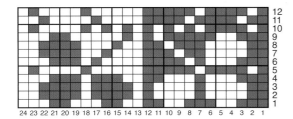

Large Sock Pattern Chart

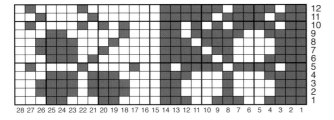

Extra Large Sock Pattern Chart

Sweetheart Knee-Highs

The inspiration for this pattern comes from Nordic carved wooden objects, such as boxes found in museums and in my family collection. Often, the boxes were carved by a young man for his sweetheart. The shaping in this pattern is done with striping down each side. The instep pattern is not symmetrical to reflect the tradition of these carvings.

SIZE

Small/Medium (Large, Extra Large)

FINISHED MEASUREMENTS

To fit foot up to an 8" (8½", 9") (20.5cm [21.5cm, 23cm]) circumference

YARN

2 (1¾oz./50g, 180yd./165m) skeins fingering weight yarn, 1 each of 2 colors (MC and CC)

The knee-highs shown here were made using Schoolhouse Press Satakieli (100% wool, 1¾oz./50g, 180yd./165m) in colors #003 Cream (MC) and #385 Brown (CC).

NEEDLES

Set of 5 US 3 (3mm) dpns or 2 circular needles, or size needed to obtain gauge

Set of 5 dpns or 2 circular needles 1 size smaller

NOTIONS

Stitch markers

Yarn needle

GAUGE

18 sts = 2" (5cm) in patt, after blocking

LEG

Using long-tail cast on, smaller needles and CC, CO 92 (96, 100) sts. Join in a rnd, being careful not to twist sts. Work in k2, p2 rib for 1¾" (4.5cm). Change to larger needles. Knit 1 rnd, inc 2 (2, 2) sts evenly around—94 (98, 102) sts. Work all rnds of Chart 1, and, on last rnd, work as follows:

K35 (37, 39), pm, k12 (shaping area), pm, k35 (37, 39), pm, k12 (shaping area).

Next rnd: *Work Rnd 1 of Chart 2 over 35 (37, 39) sts, over next 12 sts work **MC, k1; CC, k1; rep from ** to marker; rep from * once more.

Work in patt as established for 12½" (32cm), and, AT THE SAME TIME, dec in shaping areas as follows:

On 10th rnd and every following 12th round until 2 shaping sts rem in each area, in shaping areas work with CC, ssk; work in stripe patt to last 2 sts, with CC, k2tog. On last dec rnd, work k3tog using the 2 rem shaping sts and last st of chart rep—70 (74, 78) sts.

Chart 1 (above)

Chart 2 (below)

Knit all stitches for size extra large only. For size large, omit stitches 30 and 38. For size small/medium, omit stitches 30, 31, 37 and 38.

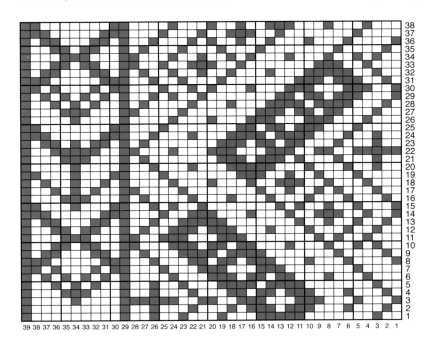

Heel Flap

First 34 (36, 38) sts are worked for Heel. Place rem 36 (38, 40) sts on hold for Instep. With RS facing, join MC and knit across Heel sts.

Set up Row (RS): Slide work back to beg of needle. With CC, *sl 1, k1; rep from * across.

Row 1 (WS): Both yarns are now at same end of needle. With MC, *sl 1, p1; rep from * across.

Row 2 (WS): Slide work back to beg of needle. With CC, purl across.

Row 3: Both yarns are now at same end of needle. With MC, *sl 1, k1; rep from * across.

Row 4: Slide work back to beg of needle. With CC, knit across.

Rep Rows 1–4 a total of 6 (7, 7) times, then work Rows 1–2 again 1 (0, 1) time more. Break off CC.

Turn Heel

Row 1 (RS): K18 (19, 20), ssk, k1, turn.

Row 2: Sl 1, p3, p2tog, p1, turn.

Row 3: Sl 1, k4, ssk, k1, turn.

Row 4: Sl 1, p5, p2tog, p1, turn.

Cont in this manner, working 1 more st before dec each row until all sts have been worked—18 (20, 20) sts. Break yarn.

Gusset

With MC, pick up and knit 14 (15, 16) sts along side of Heel Flap, knit across Heel sts, pick up and knit 14 (15, 16) sts along opposite side of Heel Flap—46 (50, 52) sts. Pm 5 (6, 6) sts in from each end of Heel sts.

Rnd 1: Work Instep chart across 36 (38, 40) Instep sts, maintaining patt; on Heel sts work *with MC, k1; with CC, k1; rep from * to marker, knit Heel Chart over next 36 (38, 40) Heel sts, *with CC, k1; with MC, k1; rep from * to end.

Rnd 2: Work Instep sts in patt; on Heel sts work with MC, ssk; work in patt to last 2 sts, with MC, k2tog.

Rep Rnds 1–2 until 36 (38, 40) Heel sts rem—72 (76, 80) sts. Work even in patt until piece measures 2½" (6.5cm) less than desired length.

Toe

With MC, knit 1 rnd.

Next rnd: *With MC, k1; with CC, k1; rep from * around.

Rnd 1: With MC, k2; knit across Instep, working opposite color in each st as worked on previous row to last 2 sts, with MC, k2; rep across Heel sts.

Rnd 2: With MC, k1, ssk; work in patt to last 3 sts, with MC, k2tog, k1; rep across Heel sts.

Rep Rnds 1–2 until 34 (34, 34) sts rem. Rep Rnd 2 until 22 (22, 22) sts rem.

Finishing

Graft Toe using Kitchener stitch. Weave in ends.

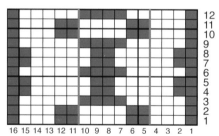

Heel Chart (above)

For size extra large, knit sts 1–4, then rep sts 5–10 until 6 sts rem, then knit sts 11–16. For size large, do the same, but omit sts 2 and 15. For size small/medium, omit sts 2, 3, 14 and 15.

Instep Chart (at right)

Knit all stitches for size extra large only. For size large, omit stitches 31 and 39. For size small/medium, omit stitches 31, 32, 38 and 39.

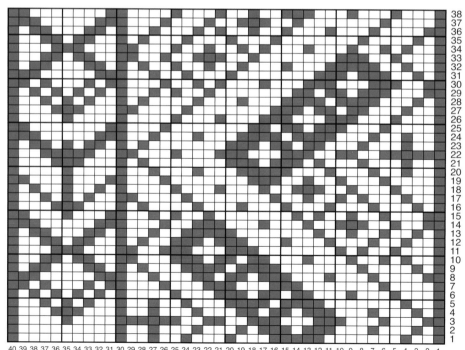

Sweetheart Socks

Using yarns with less contrast gives these socks a calmer appearance. This pair features different yarn requirements than the knee-highs.

YARN

2 (1³/₄oz./50g, 180yd./165m) skeins fingering weight yarn, 1 each of 2 colors (MC and CC)

LEG

Using long-tail cast on, smaller needles and CC, CO 68 (72, 76) sts. Join in a rnd, being careful not to twist sts. Work in k2, p2 rib for 1³/₄" (4.5cm). Change to larger needles. Knit 1 rnd, inc 2 (2, 2) sts evenly around—70 (74, 78) sts. Follow Chart 1 (page 51) once, then follow Chart 2 (page 51) until the piece measures 8" (20.5cm) or desired length. Finish Sock as for Knee-High from Heel Flap to Finishing, using Sock Instep Chart instead of Instep Chart.

The socks shown here were made using Rauma Finullgarn (100% Norwegian 2-ply wool, 1³/₄oz./50g, 180yd./165m) in colors #422 Brown (MC) and #419 Rust (CC).

Sock Instep Chart

Knit all stitches for size extra large only. For size large, omit stitches 5 and 36. For size small/medium, omit stitches 4, 5, 36 and 37.

38 37 36 35 34 33 32 31 30 29 28 27 26 25 24 23 22 21 20 19 18 17 16 15 14 13 12 11 10 9 8 7 6 5 4 3 2 1

40 39 38 37 36 35 34 33 32 31 30 29 28 27 26 25 24 23 22 21 20 19 18 17 16 15 14 13 12 11 10 9 8 7 6 5 4 3 2 1

Art Deco Knee-Highs

I have always been a fan of Art Deco, a style of design that was popular in the 1920s and 1930s that is marked by stylized forms and geometric designs. This design was adapted from an old mirror and a length of fabric. The pattern has almost a *trompe l'oeil* flavor and can look very different depending on the colors used.

The shaping runs down each side, using stripes to accentuate the crispness of the stranded pattern. This striping is carried forward in a different stitch on the heel and the toe by employing a swing needle approach, so only one color yarn is used at a time.

SIZE

Small/Medium (Large, Extra Large)

FINISHED MEASUREMENTS

To fit foot up to an 8" (8½", 9") (20.5cm [21.5cm, 23cm]) circumference

YARN

2 (1¾oz./50g, 180yd./165m) skeins fingering weight yarn, 1 each of 2 colors (MC and CC)

The knee-highs shown here were made using Dale Baby Ull (100% merino wool, 1¾oz./50g, 180yd./165m) in colors #5226 Lilac (MC) and #0020 Natural (CC).

NEEDLES

Set of 5 US 3 (3mm) dpns or 2 circular needles, or size needed to obtain gauge
Set of 5 dpns or 2 circular needles 1 size smaller

NOTIONS

Stitch markers
Yarn needle

GAUGE

17 sts = 2" (5cm) in patt, after blocking

LEG

Using long-tail cast on, smaller needles and CC, CO 93 (96, 99) sts. Join in a rnd, being careful not to twist sts. Work in k2, p1 rib as follows:

With CC, 1 rnd.

With MC, 9 rnds.

With CC, 2 rnds.

With MC, 2 rnds.

With CC, 3 rnds.

Change to larger needles and knit 1 rnd in CC, inc 3 (4, 5) sts evenly, placing markers after the first 13 sts, after the next 35 (37, 39) sts, and after the next 13 sts—96 (100, 104) sts. Shaping is worked in the 13-st sections.

Rnd 1: **With CC, k1, work Pattern Chart (page 56) across 33 (35, 37) sts, with CC, k1; over 13-st shaping section work as follows: *with CC, k1, with MC, k1; rep from * across shaping section, end with CC, k1. Rep from ** once to complete rnd. Cont as established until piece measures 12½" (32cm), and, AT THE SAME TIME, shape as follows:

On shaping sections only, on 10th rnd and every following 12th rnd until 70 (74, 78) sts rem: with CC, ssk, work as set across shaping section to last 2 sts before marker, with CC, k2tog.

HEEL FLAP

Row 1 (RS): With CC, knit across 35 (37, 39) sts, place rem 35 (37, 39) sts on hold for Instep.

Row 2 (RS): Slide work back to beg of needle. With MC, *sl 1, k1; rep from * to last st, sl 1.

Row 3 (WS): Both yarns are now at same end of needle. With CC, purl across.

Row 4 (WS): Slide work back to beg of needle. With MC, *sl 1, p1; rep from * across, sl 1. Both yarns are now at same end of needle.

Rep Rows 1–4 8 (9, 10) times more, then work Rows 1–2 once more, inc 1 st on Row 2—36 (38, 40) sts. Break off CC.

Purl back with MC.

TURN HEEL

Row 1 (RS): K18 (19, 20), ssk, k1, turn.

Row 2: Sl 1, p1, p2tog, k1, turn.

Row 3: Sl 1 pwise, knit to 1 st before gap, ssk, k1, turn.

Row 4: Sl 1 pwise, knit to 1 st before gap, k2tog, k1, turn.

Rep Rows 3–4 until all sts have been worked—18 (19, 20) sts.

Break yarn.

Join yarn at end of Instep, and with MC, pick up and knit 17 (18, 21) sts along side of Heel Flap, knit across 18 (19, 20) Heel sts, dec 1 (0, 1) st evenly across, pick up and knit 17 (18, 21) sts along opposite side of Heel Flap—51 (55, 61) sts, excluding Instep sts.

Join CC and work across Instep sts in patt.

Rnd 1: *With CC, k1, with MC, k1; rep from * across Heel, ending with CC, k1; work Instep sts in patt.

Rnd 2: With CC, ssk, work in stripe patt across Heel to last 2 sts, with CC, k2tog; work Instep sts in patt.

Rep Rnds 1–2 until 70 (74, 78) sts rem. Work even in patt until piece measures 2" (5cm) less than desired length. Knit 1 rnd in CC.

TOE

Rnd 1: With MC, *k1, sl 1; rep from * across Heel sts, ending with k1. Rep across Instep.

Rnds 2 and 4: With CC, k1, ssk, knit across Heel to last 3 sts, k2tog, k1. Rep across Instep.

Rnd 3: With MC, k1, *k1, sl 1; rep from * across Heel sts, ending with k2. Rep across Instep.

Rep Rnds 1–4 until 26 sts rem.

FINISHING

Graft Toe using Kitchener stitch. Weave in ends.

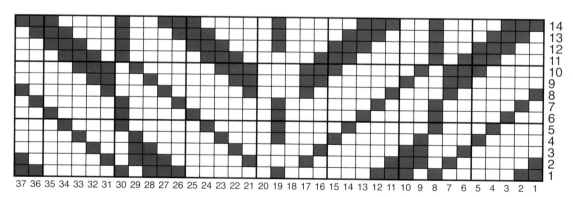

Pattern Chart

Knit all stitches for size extra large only. For size large, omit stitches 1 and 37. For size small/medium, omit stitches 1, 2, 36 and 37.

Art Deco Socks

Try switching the values of your main color and contrasting color to emphasize the different parts of this design, or choose yarns of similar values for a more subtle look.

LEG

With smaller needles and CC, CO 69 (75, 78) sts. Join in a rnd, being careful not to twist sts. Work in k2, p1 rib as follows:

With CC, 1 rnd.

With MC, 9 rnds.

With CC, 2 rnds.

With MC, 2 rnds.

With CC, 3 rnds.

Change to larger needles and knit 1 rnd in CC, inc 1 (0, 0) st evenly, and dec 0 (1, 0) sts—70 (74, 78) sts.

Rnd 1: *With CC, k1, work Pattern Chart (page 56) across 33 (35, 37) sts, with CC, k1; rep from * once to complete rnd. Cont as established until piece measures 8" (20.5cm). Finish Sock as for Knee-High from Heel Flap to Finishing.

The socks shown above were made using Dale Baby Ull (100% merino wool, 1³/₄oz./50g, 180yd./165m) in colors #5726 Bright Blue (MC) and #3871 Brown (CC). The sock below was made using Sandnessgarn Sisu (80% wool/20%nylon, 1³/₄oz./50g, 175yd./160m) in colors 1099 Black (MC) and 4715 Pink (CC).

57

Flora Knee-Highs

The Swedish ladies in the neighborhood I grew up in loved to knit big, bright flowers on sweaters and hats. They never worried about the number of stitches they were carrying the yarn across, but because these flowers will be on socks, make sure to twist the yarn every five stitches or so so you don't catch a toe in the yarn when you're putting them on! The shaping in these knee-highs is done in a panel down the back of the sock.

SIZE

Small/Medium (Large, Extra Large)

FINISHED MEASUREMENTS

To fit foot up to an 8" (8½", 9") (20.5cm [21.5cm, 23cm]) circumference

YARN

2 (1¾oz./50g, 185yd./169m) skeins fingering weight yarn, 1 each of 2 colors (MC and CC)

The knee-highs shown here were made using Van Der Rock Super Sock (100% superwash merino wool, 1¾oz./50g, 185yd./169m) in colors Lead (MC) and Tartrazine (CC).

NEEDLES

Set of 5 US 3 (3mm) dpns or 2 circular needles, or size needed to obtain gauge

Set of 5 dpns or 2 circular needles 1 size smaller

NOTIONS

Stitch markers

Yarn needle

GAUGE

17 sts = 2" (5cm) in patt, after blocking

LEG

Using long-tail cast on, smaller needles and CC, CO 93 (96, 99) sts. Join in a rnd, being careful not to twist sts. Work 2 rounds k2, p1 ribbing. Change to MC and work 18 rounds k2, p1 ribbing. Change to larger needles. Knit 1 rnd, inc 1 (2, 3) st—94 (98, 102) sts. Pm after first 30 (30, 31) sts (shaping area).

Work Shaping Chart (page 62) on first 30 (30, 31) sts and appropriate Flower Chart for your size (page 60) on rem 64 (68, 71) sts.

When shaping is complete, cont in patt as established, working even in patt until piece measures 13" (33cm). Break yarn.

HEEL FLAP

Place the first 18 (19, 20) sts and the last 15 (16, 17) sts of rnd on one needle for Heel Flap—33 (35, 37) sts. Place rem 35 (37, 39) sts on hold for Instep. Join CC. Knit 1 row, inc 1 (1, 1) st—34 (36, 38) sts.

Row 1 (WS): Sl 1, purl to end.

Row 2: *Sl 1, k1; rep from * across.

Rep Rows 1–2 a total of 14 (15, 16) times, then work Row 1 once more.

TURN HEEL

Row 1 (RS): K18 (19, 20), ssk, k1, turn.

Row 2: Sl 1, p3, p2tog, p1, turn.

Row 3: Sl 1, k4, ssk, k1, turn.

Row 4: Sl 1, p5, p2tog, p1, turn.

Cont in this manner, working 1 more st before dec each row until all sts have been worked—18 (20, 20) sts. Break yarn.

GUSSET

With MC, pick up and knit 14 (15, 16) sts along side of Heel Flap. Knit across Heel sts, dec 1 st. Pick up and knit 14 (15, 16) sts along opposite side of Heel Flap—45 (49, 51) Heel sts.

Rnd 1: Work 35 (37, 39) Instep sts in patt (see note with chart on page 60 regarding Instep); over Heel sts *with MC, k1; with CC, k1; rep from * to end.

Rnd 2: Work Instep sts in patt; over Heel sts work with MC, ssk; work in stripe patt to last 2 sts, with MC, k2tog.

Rep Rnds 1–2 until 35 (37, 39) Heel sts rem. Work even in patt until piece measures 2½" (6.5cm) less than desired length.

TOE

With CC, knit 1 rnd.

Rnd 1: K1, ssk, knit to last 3 sts, k2tog, k1; rep across Heel sts.

Rnd 2: Knit.

Rep Rnds 1–2 until 24 (24, 24) sts rem.

FINISHING

Graft Toe using Kitchener stitch. Weave in ends.

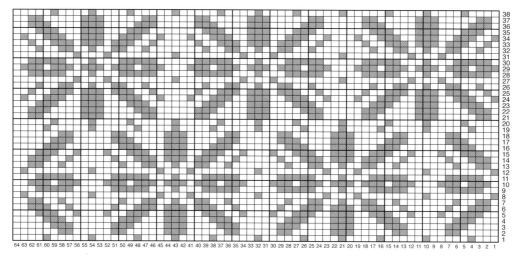

Small/Medium Flower Chart

Work stitches 15–49 only for Instep.

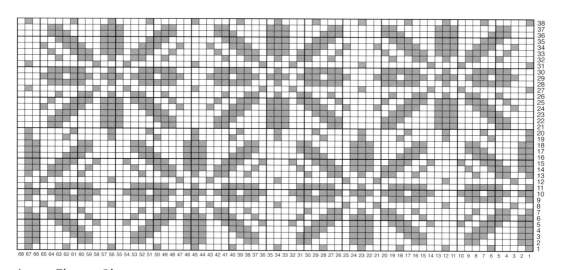

Large Flower Chart

Work stitches 16–52 only for Instep.

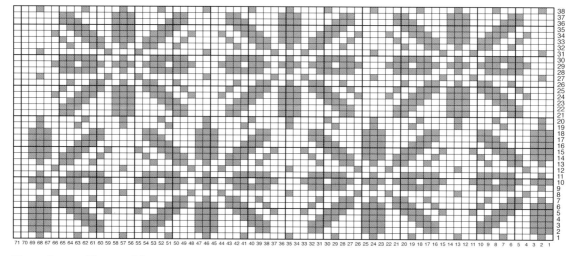

Extra Large Flower Chart

Work stitches 16–54 only for Instep.

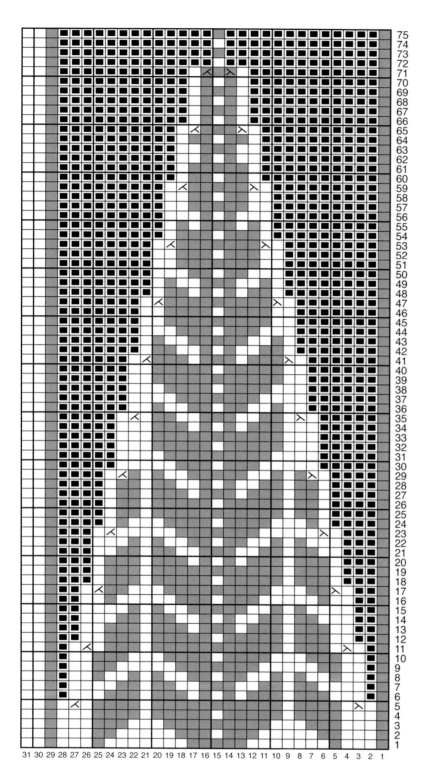

75 74 73 72 71 70 69 68 67 66 65 64 63 62 61 60 59 58 57 56 55 54 53 52 51 50 49 48 47 46 45 44 43 42 41 40 39 38 37 36 35 34 33 32 31 30 29 28 27 26 25 24 23 22 21 20 19 18 17 16 15 14 13 12 11 10 9 8 7 6 5 4 3 2 1

31 30 29 28 27 26 25 24 23 22 21 20 19 18 17 16 15 14 13 12 11 10 9 8 7 6 5 4 3 2 1

Shaping Chart

Knit all stitches for size extra large only. For sizes large and small/medium, omit stitch 31.

Flora Socks

Whether this pattern is worked with high contrast or low, the flowers still show beautifully. This sock features different yarn requirements than the knee-high.

YARN

2 (3½oz./100g, 430yd./393m) skeins fingering weight yarn, 1 each of 2 colors (MC and CC)

LEG

With smaller needles and CC, CO 66 (72, 75) sts. Join in a rnd, being careful not to twist sts. Work in k2, p1 rib for 1½" (4cm). Change to larger needles. Knit 1 rnd, inc 2 (0, 1) sts evenly around—68 (72, 76) sts. Following the appropriate Flower Chart for your size (page 60), beg with Rnd 1 and work until piece measures approx 7" (18cm). Finish Sock as for Knee-High from Heel Flap to Finishing, working toe in MC.

The sock shown here was made using Three Irish Girls Adorn Sock (80% merino wool/20% nylon, 3½oz./100g, 430yd./393m) in colors Olive Grove (MC) and Blue Divinity (CC).

Airy Mountain Knee-Highs

The inspiration for these socks came from "The Fairies," a poem by William Allingham. The beginning reads, "Up the airy mountain, down the rushy glen..." The picture this paints for me is one of ferns, shadows and lacy leaves.

The fern stitch used here is a variation my mother used often. It is a common stitch throughout Shetland and Northern Europe, with slight differences from region to region. The shaping for this pair is worked up the back of the leg in a garter stitch band with flowers. The picot cast on adds a frilly touch, as does the stem stitch used on the heel and toe. This stitch is quite stretchy, so it is a good pattern for gift giving when you are not completely sure of the recipient's measurements.

SIZE

Small/Medium (Large, Extra Large)

FINISHED MEASUREMENTS

To fit foot up to an 8" (8½", 9") (20.5cm [21.5cm, 23cm]) circumference

YARN

2 (3½oz./100g, 459yd./420m) skeins fingering weight yarn

The knee-highs shown here were made using Zitron Trekking Pro Natura (75% wool/25% unprocessed bamboo, 3½oz./100g, 459yd./420m) in color #1602 Herbs.

NEEDLES

Set of 5 US 2 (2.75mm) dpns or 2 circular needles, or size needed to obtain gauge

NOTIONS

Stitch markers
Yarn needle

GAUGE

18 sts = 2" (5cm) in patt, after blocking

Picot Cast On

*CO 5 sts using the knitted cast on. BO 2 sts, sl the rem st on the right needle to the left needle; rep from * until the desired number of sts are cast on.

LEG

Using Picot Cast On, CO 93 (96, 99) sts.

Purl 1 row. Join in a rnd, being careful not to twist sts. Knit 1 rnd.

Work 18 rnds of k2, p1 rib. Knit 1 rnd, inc 0 (0, 1) sts and dec 1 (1, 0) st—92 (95, 100) sts. AT THE SAME TIME, place markers as follows: k52 (54, 58), pm, p22, pm, k18 (19, 20). The 22 sts between markers are for the shaping area at the back of the calf. Beg with Rnd 1, follow the appropriate Pattern Chart for your size (page 67) over 52 (54, 58) sts (note: 3rd rep of patt will be incomplete), sm, work Rnd 1 of appropriate Shaping Chart for your size (page 66) over next 22 sts, sm, work appropriate Pattern Chart to end of rnd. Work in patt until piece measures approx 13" (33cm). When charts are complete, there will be 72 (76, 80) sts.

Note: Only pattern rows are charted. Knit every other row plain. Also, double yarn overs are worked k1, p1 in following rnd.

HEEL FLAP

Knit across first 35 (37, 39) sts of rnd and move the last 1 (2, 1) st of rnd onto the same needle for the Heel Flap—36, (39, 40) sts.

Place rem 36 (37, 40) sts on hold for Instep.

With WS facing, knit across Heel Flap sts, dec 0 (1, 0) sts—36 (38, 40) sts on Heel Flap.

Row 1 (RS): Sl 1, knit to end of row.

Row 2: Sl 1, *k1, sl 1 wyib; rep from * to last st, k1.

Rep these 2 rows a total of 16 (18, 20) times.

TURN HEEL

Row 1 (RS): K18 (19, 20), ssk, k1, turn.

Row 2: Sl 1, k1, k2tog, k1, turn.

Row 3: Sl 1 pwise, knit to 1 st before gap, ssk, k1, turn.

Row 4: Sl 1 pwise, knit to 1 st before gap, k2tog, k1, turn.

Rep Rows 3-4 until all sts have been worked—18 (19, 20) sts.

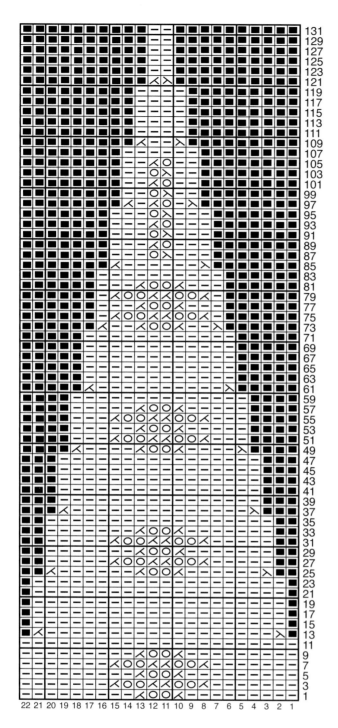

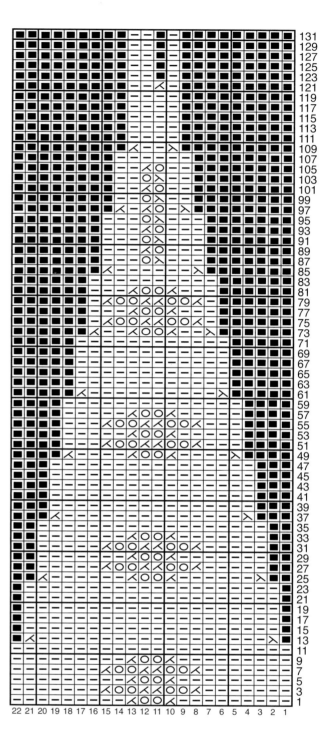

Shaping Chart (Sizes Small/Medium and Extra Large)

Only pattern rows are charted. Knit every other row plain.
Note: Double yarn overs are worked k1, p1 in following rnd.

Shaping Chart (Size Large)

Only pattern rows are charted. Knit every other row plain.
Note: Double yarn overs are worked k1, p1 in following rnd.

66

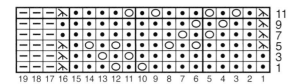

Pattern Chart (Sizes Small/Medium and Large)

Only pattern rows are charted. Knit every other row plain. Knit all stitches for size large. For size small/medium, omit stitch 18.

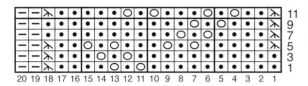

Pattern Chart (Size Extra Large)

Only pattern rows are charted. Knit every other row plain.

GUSSET

Rnd 1: Pick up and knit 17 (19, 21) sts along side of Heel Flap. Across Instep sts, p1, work 2 reps of patt, p1. Pick up and knit 17 (19, 21) sts along opposite side of Heel Flap, knit across Heel sts—88 (94, 102) sts.

Rnd 2: Knit, maintaining patt on Instep.

Next rnd: Knit to last 3 sts before Instep, k2tog, k1. Work in patt across Instep, k1, ssk, knit to end of rnd.

Next rnd: Work even in patt.

Rep last 2 rnds until 72 (77, 80) sts rem. Work even in patt until piece measures 1¼" (3cm) less than desired length.

TOE

Set up Rnd (size large only): Work 1 rnd, dec 3 sts evenly on heel—72 (74, 80) sts.

Rnd 1: *Sl 1 wyif, p1; rep from * to last 3 sts before Instep, p2tog, p1; across Instep work p1, p2tog, *sl 1 wyif, p1; rep from * to last 3 sts of Instep, p2tog, p1; p1, p2tog, *p1, sl 1 wyif; rep from * to end.

Rnds 2 and 4: Knit.

Rnd 3: *Sl 1 wyif, p1; rep from * to last 3 sts before Instep, p2tog, p1; across Instep work p1, p2tog; *p1, sl 1 wyif; rep from * to last 3 sts of Instep, p2tog, p1; p1, p2tog, *sl 1 wyif, p1; rep from * to end.

Rep Rnds 1–4 until 20 (22, 24) sts rem, ending with Rnd 2 or 4.

FINISHING

Graft Toe using Kitchener stitch. Weave in ends.

Airy Mountain Socks

This adaptation of the knee-high pattern is just as airy and feminine. The amount of yarn used varies from the knee-highs.

YARN

1 (3½oz./100g, 459yd./420m) skein fingering weight yarn

LEG

Using Picot Cast On, CO 72 (75, 81) sts.

Purl 1 row. Join in a rnd, being careful not to twist sts. Knit 1 rnd.

Work 14 rnds of k2, p1 rib. Knit 1 rnd, inc 0 (1, 0) sts and dec 0 (0, 1) sts—72 (76, 80) sts. Follow appropriate Pattern Chart (page 67), beg with Rnd 1; work until piece measures approx 7" (18cm), ending with a plain knit row. Finish Sock as for Knee-High from Heel Flap to Finishing.

The socks shown here were made using Zitron Trekking Pro Natura (75% wool/25% unprocessed bamboo, 3½oz./100g, 459yd./420m) in color #1546 Ripe Peach.

Czarina's Lace Knee-Highs

This pattern is based on a lace stitch shown to my family by Mrs. Katya, who was from Siberia. It seems to be a version of Oriel Lace, but with a different middle decrease. The shaping for these knee-highs is done within the lace panel—a yarn over is omitted where decreases are planned.

SIZE

Small/Medium (Large, Extra Large)

FINISHED MEASUREMENTS

To fit foot up to an 8" (9", 10") (20.5cm [23cm, 25.5cm]) circumference

YARN

1 (4½oz./127g, 360yd./329m) skein fingering weight yarn

The knee-highs shown here were made using Blue Moon Fiber Arts Socks That Rock Lightweight (100% superwash merino wool, 4½oz./127g, 360yd./329m) in color Gale's Autumn Joy.

NEEDLES

Set of 5 US 2 (2.75mm) dpns or 2 circular needles, or size needed to obtain gauge

NOTIONS

Stitch markers
Yarn needle

GAUGE

17 sts = 2" (5cm) in patt, after blocking

LEG

Using long-tail cast on, CO 92 (100, 108) sts. Join in a rnd, being careful not to twist sts. Work in k1, p1 rib for 2" (5cm).

Work all rnds of 23- (25-, 27-) Stitch Decrease Chart (pages 72–73) once—84 (92, 100) sts.

Work all rnds of 21- (23-, 25-) Stitch Plain Chart (pages 72–73) once.

Work all rnds of 21- (23-, 25-) Stitch Decrease Chart (pages 72–73) once—76 (84, 92) sts.

Work all rnds of 19- (21-, 23-) Stitch Plain Chart (pages 73–74) once.

Work all rnds of 19- (21-, 23-) Stitch Decrease Chart (pages 73–74) once—68 (76, 84) sts.

Work even in patt until piece measures 13" (33cm).

HEEL FLAP

Use first 34 (38, 42) sts for Heel. Place rem 34 (38, 42) sts on hold for Instep.

Row 1 (RS): *Sl 1, k1; rep from * across.

Row 2: Sl 1, purl to end.

Rep Rows 1–2 a total of 17 (18, 19) times.

TURN HEEL

Row 1 (RS): K18 (19, 22), ssk, k1, turn.

Row 2: Sl 1, p3, p2tog, p1, turn.

Row 3: Sl 1, k4, ssk, k1, turn.

Row 4: Sl 1, p5, p2tog, p1, turn.

Cont as established, working 1 more st before dec each row until all sts have been worked—18 (20, 22) sts.

GUSSET

Knit across Heel sts. Pick up and knit 17 (18, 19) sts along side of Heel Flap. Work in patt across Instep. Pick up and knit 17 (18, 19) sts along opposite side of Heel Flap. Work to center of Heel to mark new beg of rnd—86 (94, 102) sts.

Rnd 1: Knit to last 3 sts of Gusset, k2tog, k1; work Instep sts in patt; k1, ssk, knit to end of rnd.

Rnd 2: Work even in patt.

Rep Rnds 1–2 until 68 (76, 84) sts rem. Work even until piece measures 2" (5cm) less than desired length.

TOE

Knit 1 rnd.

Rnd 1: *K1, sl 1; rep from * to last 3 Heel sts, k2tog, k1; across Instep work k1, ssk, *k1, sl 1; rep from * to last 3 sts, k2tog, k1; k1, ssk, *k1, sl 1; rep from * to end.

Rnds 2 and 4: Knit.

Rnd 3: *Sl 1, k1; rep from * to last 3 Heel sts, k2tog, k1; work as for Rnd 1 across Instep, finish as for Rnd 1.

Rep Rnds 1–4 until 20 (24, 24) sts rem.

FINISHING

Graft Toe using Kitchener stitch. Weave in ends.

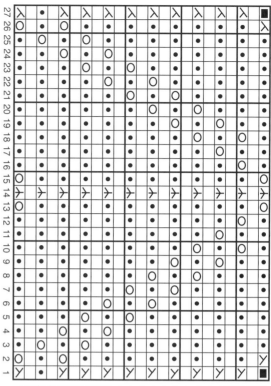

27-Stitch Decrease Chart (chart rotated to fit page)

Knit all stitches in even rounds.

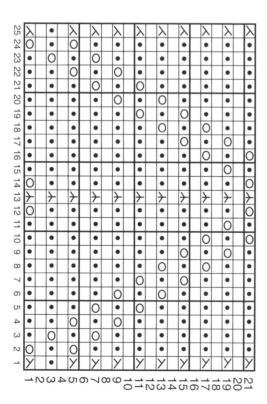

25-Stitch Plain Chart (chart rotated to fit page)

Knit all stitches in even rounds.

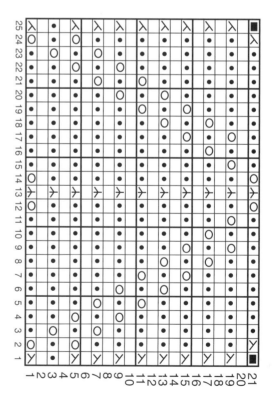

25-Stitch Decrease Chart (chart rotated to fit page)

Knit all stitches in even rounds.

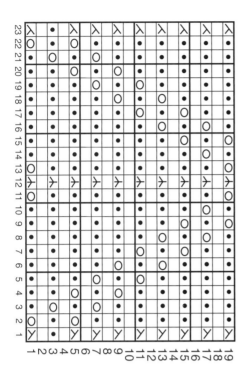

23-Stitch Plain Chart (chart rotated to fit page)

Knit all stitches in even rounds.

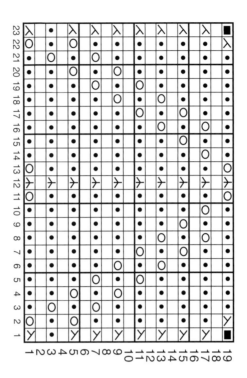

23-Stitch Decrease Chart (chart rotated to fit page)

Knit all stitches in even rounds.

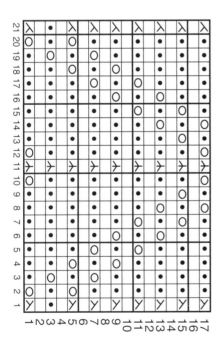

21-Stitch Plain Chart (chart rotated to fit page)

Knit all stitches in even rounds.

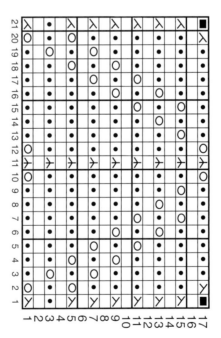

21-Stitch Decrease Chart (chart rotated to fit page)

Knit all stitches in even rounds.

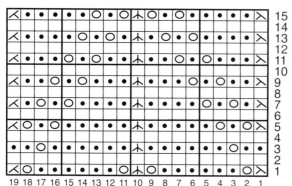

19-Stitch Plain Chart

Knit all stitches in even rounds.

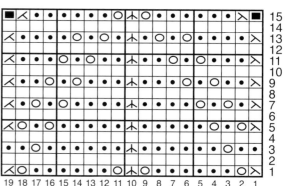

19-Stitch Decrease Chart

Knit all stitches in even rounds.

Czarina's Lace Socks and Anklets

These socks use the same materials as the knee-high. To create the ankle socks pictured, use the instructions on page 16 for converting a knee-high pattern to a Short Sock with a Turnback Cuff.

LEG

Using long-tail cast on, CO 68 (76, 84) sts. Join in a rnd, being careful not to twist sts. Work in k1, p1 rib for 1½" (4cm). Work 17- (19-, 21-) Stitch Plain Chart (pages 73–75) until piece measures approx 7" (18cm). Finish Sock as for Knee-High from Heel Flap to Finishing.

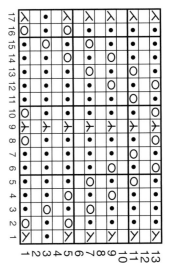

17-Stitch Plain Chart (chart rotated to fit page)

Knit all stitches in even rounds.

The socks and anklets shown on this page were made using Blue Moon Fiber Arts Socks That Rock Light-weight (100% superwash merino wool, 4½ oz./127g, 360yd./329m). The socks were made in color Barney Rubble and the anklets were made using color Knitters Without Borders.

75

Naughty and Nice Knee-Highs

The inspiration for this pattern came from the mesh stockings that have gone in and out of fashion for decades. The Stockinette stitch stripes draw the eye vertically, making the leg look long and slim. An eyelet and decrease stripe down the back of the leg imitates the seam that always appeared on these stockings. The shaping is done in Stockinette stitch down the back of the leg, emphasizing the seam. A row of eyelets around the top is worked to hold a ribbon garter under the wavy top border. Knit them in a dark color for the Naughty look, or a pretty pastel for someone Nice.

SIZE

Small/Medium (Large, Extra Large)

FINISHED MEASUREMENTS

To fit foot up to an 8½" (9", 9½") (21.5cm [23cm, 24cm]) circumference

YARN

2 (3½oz./100g, 400yd./366m) skeins fingering weight yarn

The knee-highs shown here were made using Handwerks Necessary Sock (100% superwash merino wool, 3½oz./100g, 400yd./366m) in color Berry Bramble.

NEEDLES

Set of 5 US 2 (2.75mm) dpns or 2 circular needles, or size needed to obtain gauge

Set of 5 dpns or 2 circular needles 1 size smaller

NOTIONS

Stitch markers

Yarn needle

Ribbon

GAUGE

16 sts = 2" (5cm) in patt, after blocking

LEG

Using long-tail cast on and smaller needles, CO 102 (108, 114) sts. Join in a rnd, being careful not to twist the sts. Work Rows 1–4 of Chart 1 (page 78) twice, then work Rows 1–2 once more.

Cont as follows:

Rnd 1: *K15 (16, 17), k2tog; rep from * around—96 (102, 108) sts.

Rnd 2: *K14 (15, 16), k2tog, k16 (17, 18); rep from * around—93 (99, 105) sts.

Rnds 3–13: *K2, p1; rep from * around.

Rnd 14: Purl.

Rnd 15: *K2tog, yo, p1; rep from * around.

Rnd 16: Purl.

Rnds 17–27: *K2, p1; rep from * around.

Rnd 28: K32 (34, 36), pm, k13 (14, 15) (shaping area), pm, k3 (back seam), pm, k13 (14, 15) (shaping area), pm, k30 (32, 34), k2tog—92 (98, 104) sts.

Rnd 29: K2, work Chart 2 (page 79) over next 30 sts, k 0 (2, 4), sm, k13 (14, 15), sm, yo, sl 2 tog kwise, k1, psso, yo (back seam), sm, k13 (14, 15), sm, k 0 (2, 4), work Chart 3 (page 79) over next 30 sts, k1.

Rnd 30: Knit. Work as established, maintaining seam sts and, AT THE SAME TIME, on Rnd 30 and every following 6th rnd, dec as follows until 66 (70, 74) sts rem: Work in patt to last 3 sts of shaping area, ssk, k1, work in patt across back seam, k1, k2tog at beg of next shaping area, work in patt to end. Work even in patt until piece measures 13" (33cm), ending with Rnd 2 or 4 of Chart 2.

HEEL FLAP

Break yarn.

Place first 17 (18, 19) sts and last 16 (17, 18) sts of rnd on hold for Instep. Use rem 33 (35, 37) sts for Heel Flap (seam sts are in the center). With WS facing, join yarn and purl across Heel sts, inc 1 (1, 1) st—34 (36, 38) sts.

Row 1 (RS): *Sl 1, k1; rep from * across.

Row 2: Sl 1, purl to end of row.

Rep Rows 1–2 a total of 16 (17, 18) times.

Turn Heel

Row 1 (RS): K17 (18, 19), ssk, k1, turn.

Row 2: Sl 1, p1, p2tog, p1, turn.

Row 3: Sl 1, k2, ssk, k1, turn.

Row 4: Sl 1, p3, p2tog, p1, turn.

Cont in this manner, working 1 more st before dec each row until all sts have been worked—18 (18, 20) sts.

Gusset

Knit across Heel sts, pick up and knit 16 (17, 18) sts along side of Heel Flap. On Instep, k 0 (1, 2), work Chart 3 across 30 sts, k 3 (4, 5). Pick up and knit 16 (17, 18) sts along opposite side of Heel Flap, work to center of Heel sts.

Rnd 1: Knit to last 3 Heel sts, k2tog, k1; work in patt across Instep, k1, ssk, knit to end.

Rnd 2: Work even in patt.

Rep Rnds 1–2 until 66 (70, 74) sts rem. Work even in patt until piece measures 1³/₄" (4.5cm) less than desired length.

Toe

Rnd 1: Knit to last 3 Heel sts, k2tog, k1; on Instep work k1, ssk, knit to last 3 sts, k2tog, k1; ssk, k1, knit to end of rnd.

Rnd 2: Knit.

Rep Rnds 1–2 until 22 (22, 26) sts rem.

Finishing

Graft Toe using Kitchener stitch. Weave in ends. If desired, thread ribbon through eyelets at top of knee-high and tie.

Chart 1

Knit all stitches for size extra large only. For size large, omit stitch 4. For size small/medium, omit stitches 4 and 16.

Naughty and Nice Socks

This adaptation of the knee-high pattern uses a very Nice pretty pink yarn. The amount of yarn used varies from the knee-highs.

YARN

1 (3½oz./100g, 400yd./366m) skein fingering weight yarn

LEG

Using long-tail cast on and smaller needles, CO 68 (72, 76) sts. Join in a rnd, being careful not to twist the sts. Work Rows 1–4 of Chart 1 (page 78) twice, then work Rows 1–2 once more.

Cont as follows:

Rnd 1: Knit, dec 2 (3, 1) sts evenly around—66 (69, 75) sts.

Rnd 2: Knit.

Rnds 3–13: *K2, p1; rep from * around.

Rnd 14: Purl.

Rnd 15: *K2tog, yo, p1; rep from * around.

Rnd 16: Purl.

Rnds 17–27: *K2, p1; rep from * around. On Rnd 27, inc 0 (1, 0) sts, dec 0 (0, 1) sts—66 (70, 74) sts.

Rnd 28: K32 (34, 36), pm, k3 (back seam), pm, k31 (33, 36).

Rnd 29: K2, work Chart 2 over next 30 sts, k0 (2, 4), sm, yo, sl 2 tog kwise, k1, psso, yo (back seam), sm, k0 (2, 4), work Chart 3 over next 30 sts, k1 (1, 2). Work even in patt until piece measures 8" (20.5cm), ending with Rnd 2 or 4 of Chart 2—66 (70, 74) sts.

Finish Sock as for Knee-High from Heel Flap to Finishing.

The socks shown here were made using Handwerks Necessary Sock (100% superwash merino wool, 3½oz./100g, 400yd./366m) in color Mulberries.

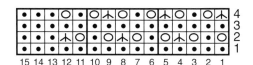

Chart 2

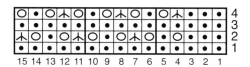

Chart 3

Davidson Road Knee-Highs

Fishermen of the Atlantic wore tightly-knit sweaters with distinctive textured patterns. Many of these patterns were created using purl stitches on a Stockinette stitch ground, and similar versions could be seen in many different villages. These knee-highs borrow those design elements and are shaped within the seed stitch stripes, giving a sophisticated and tailored look. They are suited for both men and women.

SIZE

Small/Medium (Large, Extra Large)

FINISHED MEASUREMENTS

To fit foot up to an 8" (9", 10") (20.5cm [23cm, 25.5cm]) circumference

YARN

3 (4, 4) (1¾oz./50g, 185yd./169m) skeins fingering weight yarn

The knee-highs shown here were made using Shelridge Farm Soft Touch Ultra (100% wool, 1¾oz./50g, 185yd./169m) in color Heath.

NEEDLES

Set of 5 US 1 (2.5mm) dpns or 2 circular needles, or size needed to obtain gauge

Set of 5 dpns or 2 circular needles 1 size smaller

NOTIONS

Stitch markers

Yarn needle

GAUGE

16 sts = 2" (5cm) in patt, after blocking

LEG

CO 88 (96, 104) sts. Join in a rnd, being careful not to twist sts. Work in k1, p1 rib for 2" (5cm).

Rnd 1: Knit.

Rnd 2: Purl.

Rnd 3: Knit.

Work Chart 1, then rep Rnds 1–3. Work Chart 2 (page 82). Work Chart 3 (page 84) until piece measures 13" (33cm), ending with Rnd 12—64 (72, 80) sts.

HEEL FLAP

Work in patt across 10 (11, 13) sts and place with last 21 (25, 27) sts of rnd for Heel—31 (36, 40) sts. Place rem 33 (36, 40) sts on hold for Instep. Purl 1 WS row, dec 1 (0, 0) st—30 (36, 40) sts.

Row 1 (RS): Sl 1, *k1, sl 1 wyib; rep from * to last st, k1.

Row 2: Sl 1, knit to end of row.

Rep Rows 1–2 a total of 16 (18, 20) times.

TURN HEEL

Row 1 (RS): K19 (23, 26), ssk, turn.

Row 2: Sl 1, p8 (10, 12), p2tog, turn.

Row 3: Sl 1, k8 (10, 12), ssk, turn.

Cont in this manner until all sts are worked—10 (12, 14) sts.

GUSSET

Pick up and knit 17 (19, 21) sts along side of Heel Flap, work across Instep sts as established, pick up and knit 17 (19, 21) sts along opposite side of Heel Flap, work across half of Heel sts to mark new beg of rnd—77 (86, 96) sts.

Rnd 1: Knit to 3 sts before Instep, k2tog, k1; work in patt across Instep; k1, ssk, knit to end of rnd.

Rnd 2: Work even in patt.

Rep Rnds 1–2 until 67 (72, 80) sts rem. Work even in patt until piece measures 2" (5cm) less than desired length. Dec 1 (0, 0) st on Heel sts on last rnd—66 (72, 80) sts.

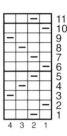

Chart 1

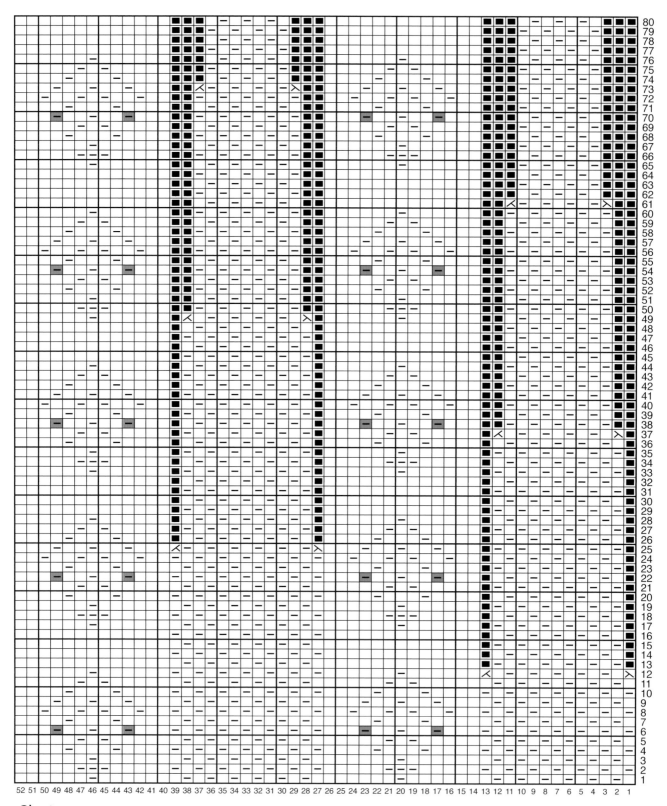

Chart 2

Knit all stitches for size extra large only. For size large, omit stitches 7-8 and 33-34. For size small/medium, omit stitches 7-8, 16, 24, 33-34, 42 and 50. The pink stitches in this chart are knit stitches for size small/medium and purl stitches for sizes large and extra large.

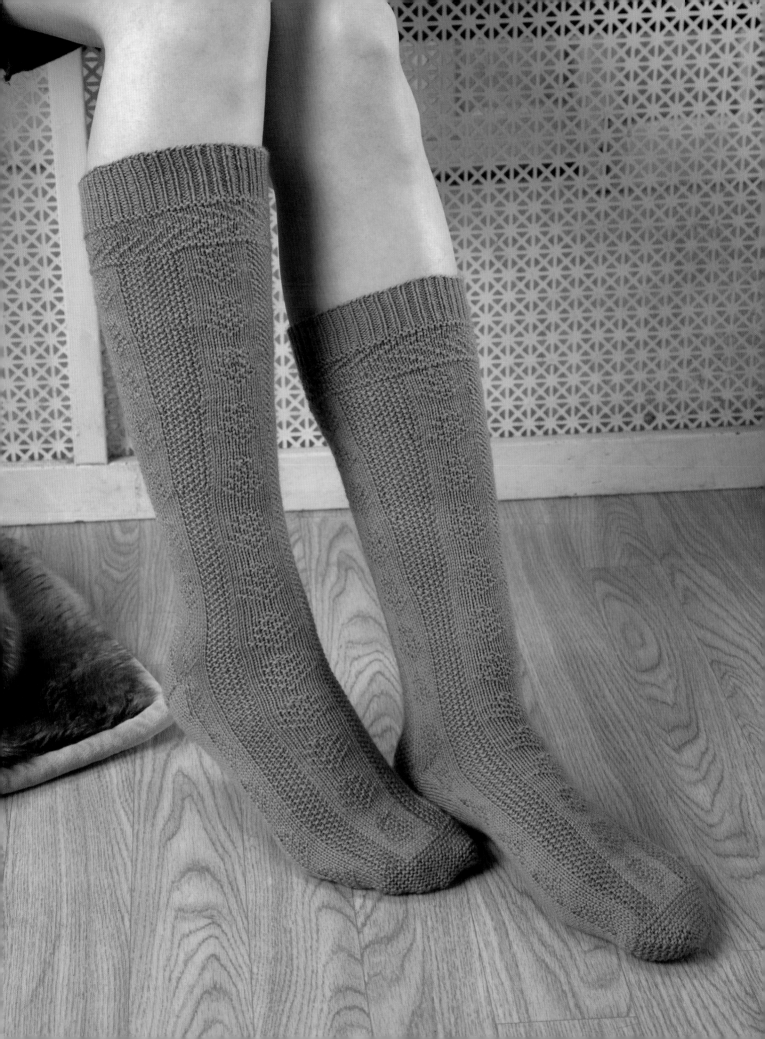

TOE

Rnd 1: *Sl 1 wyib, k1; rep from * to last 3 sts before Instep, k2tog, k1; across Instep work k1, k2tog, *sl 1 wyib, k1; rep from * to last 3 sts of Instep, k2tog, k1; k1, k2tog, *k1, sl 1 wyib; rep from * to end.

Rnds 2 and 4: Purl.

Rnd 3: *Sl 1 wyib, k1; rep from * to last 3 sts before Instep, k2tog, k1; across Instep work k1, k2tog; *k1, sl 1 wyib; rep from * to last 3 sts of Instep, k2tog, k1; k1, k2tog, *sl 1 wyib, k1; rep from * to end.

Rep Rnds 1–4 until 22 (24, 24) sts rem, ending with Rnd 2 or 4.

FINISHING

Graft Toe using Kitchener stitch. Weave in ends.

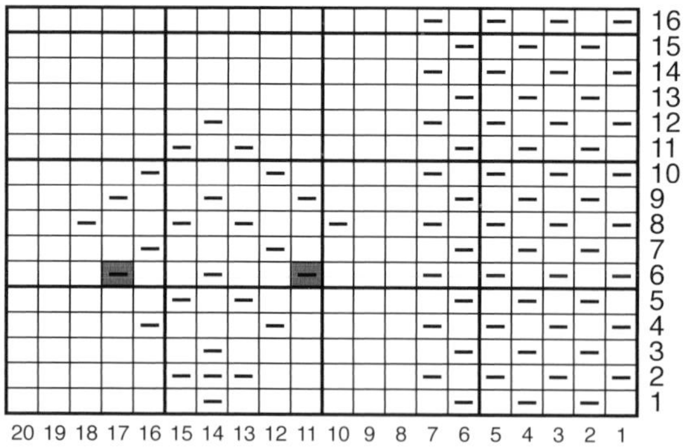

Davidson Road Socks

These socks share the sophisticated look of the knee-highs but don't need the same attention to shaping.

LEG

CO 64 (72, 80) sts. Join in a rnd, being careful not to twist sts. Work in k1, p1 rib for 2" (5cm).

Rnd 1: Knit.

Rnd 2: Purl.

Rnd 3: Knit.

Work Chart 1 (page 81), then rep Rnds 1-3. Work Chart 3 until piece measures 8" (20.5cm) or desired length, ending with Rnd 12—64 (72, 80) sts. Finish Sock as for Knee-High from Heel Flap to Finishing.

The socks shown here were made using Shelridge Farm Soft Touch Ultra (100% wool, 1³/₄oz./50g, 185yd./169m) in color Straw.

Chart 3

Knit all stitches for size extra large only. For size large, omit stitches 5–6. For size small/medium, omit stitches 5–6, 10 and 18. The pink stitches in this chart are knit stitches for size small/medium and purl stitches for sizes large and extra large.

Flutterby Knee-Highs

The old word for butterfly was "flutterby" and, in my opinion, that word describes them perfectly. These knee-highs combine a version of the butterfly stitch with a version of a stitch that was called Old Shale by the ladies in my neighborhood. The shaping is done within each pattern section.

SIZE

Small/Medium (Large, Extra Large)

FINISHED MEASUREMENTS

To fit foot up to an 8" (8½", 9") (20.5cm [21.5cm, 23cm]) circumference

YARN

2 (4oz./114g, 400yd./366m) skeins fingering weight yarn

The knee-highs shown here were made using Prairie Fibre Mill Socks. Naturally! (33.3% alpaca/33.3% merino wool/33.3% kid mohair, 4oz./114g, 400yd./366m) in color Evening Sky.

NEEDLES

Set of 5 US 2 (2.75mm) dpns or 2 circular needles, or size needed to obtain gauge

NOTIONS

Stitch markers
Yarn needle

GAUGE

17 sts = 2" (5cm) in patt, after blocking

LEG

Using long-tail cast on, CO 102 (108, 114) sts. Join in a rnd, being careful not to twist sts. [Purl 1 rnd, knit 1 rnd] twice. Work Rnds 11–20 of Chart 34 (36, 38) (pages 88–89). Work in k1, p1 rib for 9 rnds. Cont as follows (see charts on pages 88–91):

Rnds 1–20 of Chart 32 (34, 36).

Rnds 1–20 of Chart 30 (32, 34).

Rnds 1–20 of Chart 28 (30, 32).

Rnds 1–20 of Chart 26 (28, 30).

Rnds 1–20 of Chart 24 (26, 28)—66 (72, 78) sts.

Rnds 1–10 of Chart 22 (24, 26) until piece measures 13" (33cm).

HEEL FLAP

Move last 2 sts to beg of rnd, and knit across these plus next 31 (34, 37) sts—33 (36, 39) sts for Heel Flap. Place rem 33 (36, 39) sts on hold for Instep. Purl 1 row, inc 1 (0, 0) st and dec 0 (0, 1) sts—34 (36, 38) sts.

Row 1 (RS): *Sl 1, k1; rep from * to end.

Row 2: Sl 1, purl to end of row.

Rep Rows 1–2 a total of 14 (16, 18) times.

TURN HEEL

Row 1 (RS): K17 (18, 19), ssk, k1, turn.

Row 2: Sl 1, p1, p2tog, p1, turn.

Row 3: Sl 1, k2, ssk, k1, turn.

Row 4: Sl 1, p3, p2tog, p1, turn.

Cont in this manner, working 1 more st before dec each row until all sts have been worked—18 (18, 20) sts.

GUSSET

Pick up and knit 15 (17, 19) sts along side of Heel Flap, knit across Instep sts, pick up and knit 15 (17, 19) sts along opposite side of Heel Flap. Knit to center of Heel, dec 1 (0, 1) st—80 (88, 96) sts.

Rnd 1: Knit.

Rnd 2: Knit to last 3 Heel sts, k2tog, k1, knit across Instep, k1, ssk, knit to end of rnd.

Rep Rnds 1–2 until 66 (72, 78) sts rem. Work even until piece measures 2" (5cm) less than desired length.

TOE

Rnd 1: Knit to last 3 Heel sts, k2tog, k1; across Instep work k1, ssk, knit to last 3 sts, k2tog, k1; k1, ssk, knit to end of rnd.

Rnd 2: Knit.

Rep Rnds 1–2 until 34 (36, 42) sts rem. Rep Rnd 1 until 22 (24, 26) sts rem.

FINISHING

Graft Toe using Kitchener stitch. Weave in ends.

Special Symbols

⩔ slip stitch purlwise with yarn in front to create a float

♥ take the right needle underneath all 3 strands produced by the floats in the pattern rows. Knit the next stitch and come back underneath the 3 strands

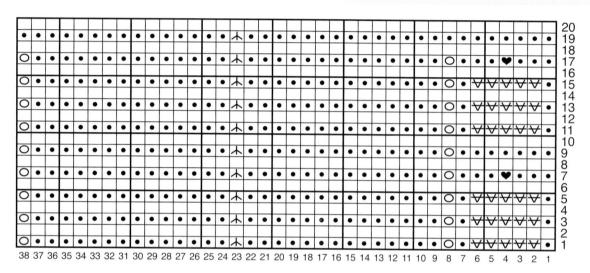

Chart 38

Knit all stitches in even rounds.

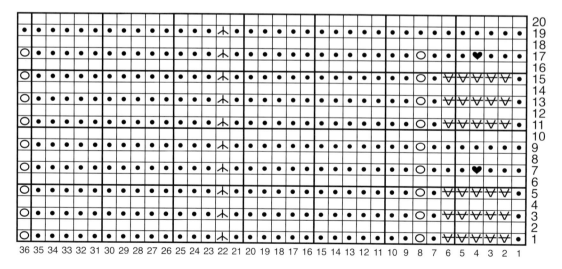

Chart 36

Knit all stitches in even rounds.

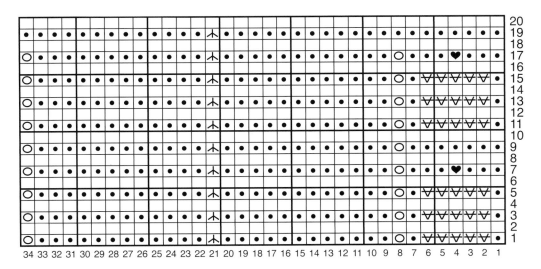

Chart 34

Knit all stitches in even rounds.

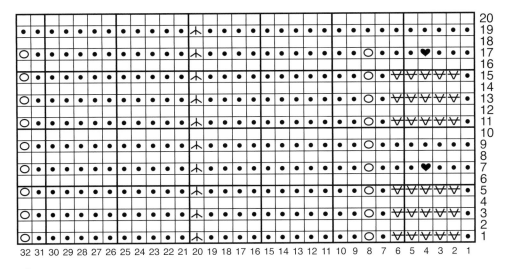

Chart 32

Knit all stitches in even rounds.

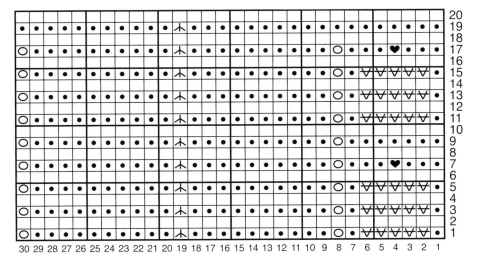

Chart 30

Knit all stitches in even rounds.

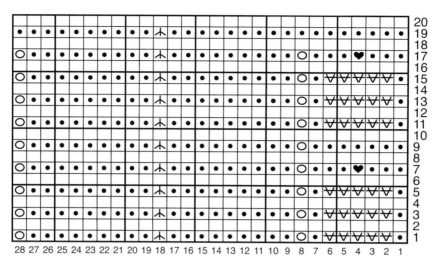

Chart 28

Knit all stitches in even rounds.

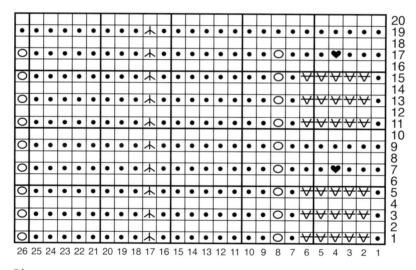

Chart 26

Knit all stitches in even rounds.

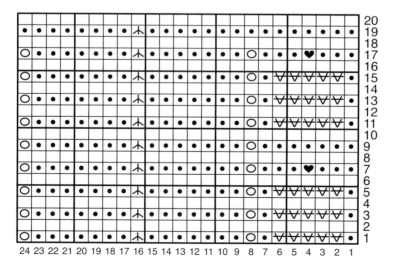

Chart 24

90

Knit all stitches in even rounds.

Flutterby Anklets

These pretty socks with turnback cuffs are a diminutive version of the knee-highs. The yarn requirements for this pair vary from the knee-highs.

YARN

1 (3½oz./100g, 400yd./366m) skein fingering weight yarn

LEG

CO 66 (72, 78) sts. Join in a rnd, being careful not to twist sts. [Purl 1 rnd, knit 1 rnd] twice. Work Rnds 1–10 of Chart 22 (24, 26) 3 times. Knit 1 rnd, then p 1 rnd for turnback. Turn work inside out for Cuff turnback and cont as follows: work in k2, p1 rib until piece measures 2" (5cm) from turnback. Finish Anklet as for Knee-High from Heel Flap to Finishing.

The anklets shown here were made using Handwerks Necessary Sock (100% superwash merino wool, 3½oz./100g, 400yd./366m) in color Sumac.

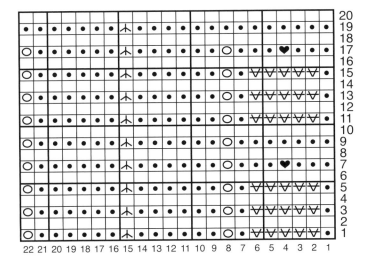

Chart 22

Knit all stitches in even rounds.

Maid Marian Knee-Highs

These knee-highs are named after Robin Hood's lady, and as such, they are dainty, delicate and lacy with a backbone of steel (the cable running down the sides). The lace is a version of Baby Horseshoe, a common lace in many North Atlantic countries. The shaping is done in a lace panel down the back.

SIZE

Small/Medium (Large, Extra Large)

FINISHED MEASUREMENTS

To fit foot up to an 8" (8½", 9") (20.5cm [21.5cm, 23cm]) circumference

YARN

1 (3½oz./100g, 400yd./366m) skein fingering weight yarn

The knee-highs shown here were made using Socks 2Dye4 (superwash merino, 3½oz./100g, 490yd./448m) in color Cream.

NEEDLES

Set of 5 US 2 (2.75mm) dpns or 2 circular needles, or size needed to obtain gauge

Set of 5 dpns or 2 circular needles 1 size smaller

NOTIONS

Cable needle

Stitch markers

Yarn needle

GAUGE

16 sts = 2" (5cm) in patt, after blocking

LEG

Using long-tail cast on and smaller needles, CO 88 (92, 96) sts. Join in a rnd, being careful not to twist the sts. Work Rnd 1 of Chart 1 (page 94), pm, (p1, k1) 13 times (shaping area), pm, work Rnd 1 of Chart 2 (page 94). Cont as established and rep Rnds 1–4 a total of 4 times, then rep Rnds 1–2 once more. Change to larger needles and knit 1 rnd.

Next rnd: Work Rnd 1 of Chart 3 (page 94), work Rnd 1 of Shaping Chart (page 94) over shaping area, work Rnd 1 of Chart 4 (page 95).

Note: In Rnd 75 of Shaping Chart, purl last st of shaping area tog with first st of Chart 4.

Cont as established. Work until piece measures 13" (33cm)—62 (66, 70) sts.

HEEL FLAP

Knit first 3 (3, 4) sts and place with last 28 (30, 31) sts on hold for Instep—31 (33, 35) sts total. Rem 31 (33, 35) sts are worked for Heel Flap.

Row 1 (RS): *Sl 1, k1; rep from * to last st, k1.

Rows 2 and 4: Sl 1, purl to end of row.

Row 3: Sl 1, k2, *sl 1, k1; rep from * to end of row.

Rep Rows 1–4 a total of 8 (9, 10) times, inc 1 st on last row—32 (34, 36) sts.

TURN HEEL

Row 1 (RS): K17, (18, 19), ssk, k1, turn.

Row 2: Sl 1, p3, p2tog, p1, turn.

Row 3: Sl 1, k4, ssk, k1, turn.

Row 4: Sl 1, p5, p2tog, p1, turn.

Cont as set, working 1 more st before dec on each row until all sts have been worked—18 (18, 20) sts.

GUSSET

Pick up and knit 17 (19, 21) sts along side of Heel Flap. Work Instep Chart across Instep sts, then pick up and knit 17 (19, 21) sts along opposite side of Heel Flap. Work to center of Heel sts, dec 1 st—82 (88, 96) sts.

Rnd 1: Knit to last 3 sts of Gusset, k2tog, k1, work in patt across Instep, k1, ssk, knit to end of rnd.

Rnd 2: Work even in patt.

Rep Rnds 1–2 until 62 (66, 70) sts rem. Work even in patt until piece measures 2" (5cm) less than desired length.

TOE

Rnd 1: *K1, sl; rep from * to last 3 Heel sts, k2tog, k1; across Instep work k1, ssk, **k1, sl 1; rep from ** to last 3 sts, k2tog, k1; across rem Heel sts work k1, ssk, ***k1, sl 1; rep from *** to end of rnd.

Rnds 2 and 4: Knit.

Rnd 3: *Sl 1, k1; rep from * to last 3 Heel sts, k2tog, k1; work as for Rnd 1 across Instep, end as for Rnd 1.

Rep Rnds 1–4 until 18 (22, 26) sts rem, ending with Rnd 2 or 4.

FINISHING

Graft Toe using Kitchener stitch. Weave in ends.

Special Symbol

sl 2 to cable needle to back, k2, k2 from cable needle

Chart 1

Knit all stitches for size extra large only. For size large, omit stitches 1 and 8. For size small/medium, omit stitches 1, 8 and 9.

Chart 3

Knit all stitches for size extra large only. For size large, omit stitches 1 and 8. For size small/medium, omit stitches 1, 8 and 9.

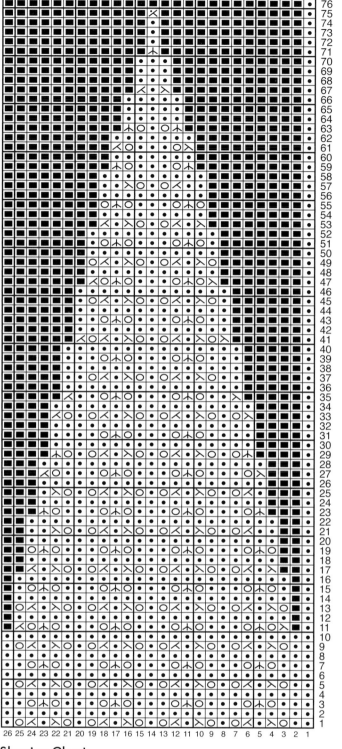

Shaping Chart

Chart 2

Knit all stitches for size extra large only. For size large, omit stitches 15 and 22. For size small/medium, omit stitches 14, 15, 22, 23 and 49.

Chart 4

Knit all stitches for size extra large only. For size large, omit stitches 15 and 22. For size small/medium, omit stitches 14, 15, 22, 23 and 49.

Instep Chart

Knit all stitches for size extra large only. For size large, omit stitches 4 and 32. For size small/medium, omit stitches 4, 5, 31 and 32.

Maid Marion Socks and Anklets

These socks use the same materials as the knee-highs, with the exception of the yarn. To create the ankle socks pictured, use the instructions on page 16 for converting a knee-high pattern to a short sock with a turnback cuff.

YARN

1 (3½oz./100g, 437yd./400m) skein fingering weight yarn

LEG

Using long-tail cast on and smaller needles, CO 62 (66, 70) sts. Join in a rnd, being careful not to twist the sts. Work Sock Chart 1 for a total of 18 rnds. Knit 2 rnds. Work Sock Chart 2 until piece measures 7" (18cm) or desired length. Finish Sock as for Knee-High from Heel Flap to Finishing.

The socks shown here were made using Cascade Heritage (75% superwash merino wool/25% nylon, 3½oz./100g, 437yd./400m) in color 5604. The anklets shown at left were made using Knit Witch Boo! (80% superwash merino wool/20% bamboo, 3½oz./100g, 435yd./398m) in color Bewitched.

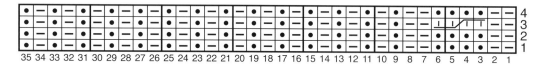

35 34 33 32 31 30 29 28 27 26 25 24 23 22 21 20 19 18 17 16 15 14 13 12 11 10 9 8 7 6 5 4 3 2 1

Sock Chart 1

Knit all stitches for size extra large only. For size large, omit stitches 1 and 8. For size small/medium, omit stitches 1, 8, 9 and 35.

35 34 33 32 31 30 29 28 27 26 25 24 23 22 21 20 19 18 17 16 15 14 13 12 11 10 9 8 7 6 5 4 3 2 1

Sock Chart 2

Knit all stitches for size extra large only. For size large, omit stitches 1 and 8. For size small/medium, omit stitches 1, 8, 9 and 35.

Counterpane Knee-Highs

Many ladies in the neighborhood I grew up in liked to knit a certain bedspread pattern. They knit it in stripes, and adapted it to squares. These knee-highs were inspired by that pattern. The shaping is done in ribbing down the back.

SIZE

Small/Medium (Large, Extra Large)

FINISHED MEASUREMENTS

To fit foot up to an 8" (8³⁄₄", 9¹⁄₂") (20.5cm [22cm, 24cm]) circumference

YARN

2 (3¹⁄₂oz./100g, 437yd./395m) skeins fingering weight yarn

The knee-highs shown here were made using Knit Witch Spellcast (50% merino wool/50% silk, 3¹⁄₂oz./100g, 437yd./395m) in color Hocus Pocus.

NEEDLES

Set of 5 US 1 (2.25mm) dpns or 2 circular needles, or size needed to obtain gauge

NOTIONS

Stitch markers
Yarn needle

GAUGE

20 sts = 2" (5cm) in patt, after blocking

LEG

Note: the stitch count does not remain constant on each row.

Using long-tail cast on, CO 112 (120, 128) sts. Join in a rnd, being careful not to twist sts. Purl 1 rnd, knit 1 rnd, purl 1 rnd.

Next rnd: K22, pm, k18 (22, 26), pm, k22, pm, knit to end.

Next rnd: Work Chart 1 on both 22-st sections, and k2, p2 rib, ending with k2, on 18- (22-, 26-) st section (front of leg) and 50- (54-, 58-) st section (back of leg), and, AT THE SAME TIME, work shaping as follows:

Work in patt and, maintaining rib patt, dec 2 sts each larger rib section (back of leg) every 12 rnds 3 times, then every 6 rnds 13 times—80 (88, 96) sts. Work in patt until piece measures 13" (33cm), ending with Rnd 6.

HEEL FLAP

Work across first 11 sts of rnd as follows: [p2, k2] twice, p3; place these sts with the last 29 (33, 37) sts of rnd for Heel—40 (44, 48) sts. Place rem 40 (44, 48) sts on hold for Instep.

Row 1 (WS): K1, *k2, p2; rep from * to last 3 sts, k3.

Row 2: K1, *p2, k2; rep from * to last 3 sts, p2, k1.

Rep Rows 1–2 a total of 15 times.

TURN HEEL

Row 1 (RS): K20 (22, 24), ssk, k1, turn.

Row 2: Sl 1, p1, p2tog, p1, turn.

Row 3: Sl 1, k2, ssk, k1, turn.

Cont in this manner, working 1 more st before dec each row until all sts have been worked—20 (22, 24) sts.

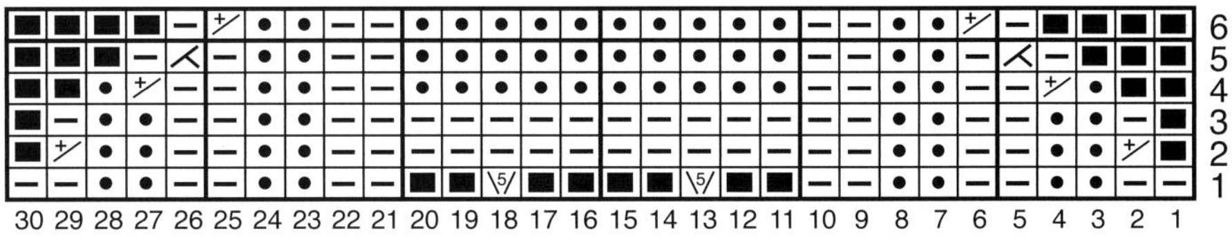

Chart 1

Special Symbol

⑤ k, p, k, p, k all in the same stitch—4 sts inc

GUSSET

Knit across Heel sts, pick up and knit 17 sts along side of Heel Flap, work Rnd 1 of Right Instep Chart, pm, [k2, p2] 4 (5, 6) times, k2, pm, work Rnd 1 of Left Instep Chart, pick up and knit 17 sts along opposite side of Heel Flap, knit to center of Heel—94 (100, 106) sts.

Work even in patt for 2 rnds.

Rnd 1: Knit to last 3 Heel sts, k2tog, k1, work in patt across Instep sts, k1, ssk, knit to end of rnd.

Rnd 2: Work even in patt.

Rep Rnds 1–2 until 80 (88, 96) sts rem. Work even in patt until piece measures 2" (5cm) less than desired length.

TOE

Knit 1 rnd.

Rnd 1: Knit to last 3 Heel sts, k2tog, k1; on Instep work k1, ssk, knit to last 3 Instep sts, k2tog, k1; k1, ssk, knit to end of rnd.

Rnd 2: Knit.

Rep Rnds 1–2 until 40 (44, 48) sts rem. Rep Rnd 1 only until 16 (20, 24) sts rem.

FINISHING

Graft Toe using Kitchener stitch. Weave in ends.

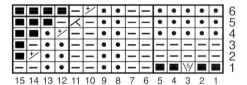

Left Instep Chart

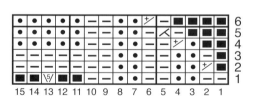

Right Instep Chart

Counterpane Socks and Legwarmers

These socks use the same materials as the knee-highs, but a different amount of yarn. To create the legwarmers pictured, use the instructions on page 17 for converting a knee-high pattern to an legwarmer pattern.

YARN

1 (3½oz./100g, 437yd./395m) skein fingering weight yarn

LEG

Using long-tail cast on, CO 80 (88, 96) sts. Join in a rnd, being careful not to twist sts. Purl 1 rnd, knit 1 rnd, purl 1 rnd.

Next rnd: K22, pm, k18 (22, 26), pm, k22, pm, knit to end. Work Chart 1 (page 99) on both 22-st sections, and k2, p2 rib, ending with k2, on both 18- (22-, 26-) st sections. Work in patt until piece measures 8" (20.5cm) or desired length, ending with Rnd 6. Finish Sock as for Knee-High from Heel Flap to Finishing.

The socks and legwarmers shown here were made using Knit Witch Spellcast (50% merino wool/50% silk, 3½oz./100g, 437yd./395m). The socks were made in color Presto and the legwarmers were made using color Abracadabra.

Stalking Stockings

At the turn of the century (19th to 20th, that is!) gentlemen wore knee-highs with their knickerbockers and plus fours, and fishermen wore (and still wear) heavy stockings in their sea boots. These, like those long-ago knee-highs, are perfect for you, or for the man in your life, whether he's a hiker, cross country skier or farmer. The turnback top is not too frilly for someone who is man enough for lace, but you can always knit the knee-high without it if you choose. The back of the leg is worked in a mock cable rib—an extremely stretchy stitch—and the shaping is worked on either side of it. This stitch carries on down into the heel flap to give extra cushioning in a work or hiking boot.

SIZES

Small/Medium (Large, Extra Large)

FINISHED MEASUREMENTS

To fit foot up to an 8½" (9", 9½") (21.5cm [23cm, 24cm]) circumference

YARN

2 (4oz./113g, 272yd./249m) skeins sport weight yarn

The knee-highs shown here were made using Briggs and Little Regal (100% wool, 4oz./113g, 272yd./249m) in color Natural White.

NEEDLES

Set of 5 US 5 (3.75mm) dpns or 2 circular needles, or size needed to obtain gauge
Set of 5 dpns or 2 circular needles 1 size smaller

NOTIONS

Stitch markers
Yarn needle

GAUGE

12 sts = 2" (5cm) in patt on larger needles, after blocking

CUFF

Using long-tail cast on and larger needles, CO 65 (70, 75) sts. Join in a rnd, being careful not to twist sts. Purl 1 rnd, knit 1 rnd, purl 1 rnd. Work Chart 1 a total of 3 times. Knit 1 rnd, purl 1 rnd. Change to smaller needles.

LEG

Turn work inside out for Cuff turnback and cont as follows:

Work in p1, k2 rib for 1 rnd, dec 2 (1, 0) sts evenly—63 (69, 75) sts.

Work in p1, k2 rib for 5 rnds.

Work in p1, k2 rib for 1 rnd, inc 1 (1, 1) st—64 (70, 76) sts.

Pm 25 (28, 31) sts from beg of rnd to mark back of sock. Rem 39 (42, 45) sts are front of sock. Change to larger needles.

Rnd 1: *P1, k2; rep from * to 1 st before marker, p1, k to end of rnd.

Rnd 2: *P1, k1, yo, k1; rep from * to 1 st before marker, p1, k to end of rnd.

Rnd 3: *P1, k3; rep from * to 1 st before marker, p1, k to end of rnd.

Rnd 4: *P1, sl 1, k2, psso; rep from * to 1 st before marker, p1, k to end of rnd.

Rep Rnds 1–4, and, AT THE SAME TIME, dec every 8 (10, 12) rnds as follows until 52 (56, 60) sts rem: Work in patt to marker, k1, k2tog, k to last 3 sts, ssk, k1.

Work even in patt until work from turnback measures 13" (33cm). On last rnd, dec 1 (0, 0) st and inc 0 (0, 1) sts on front of sock sts—51 (56, 61) sts; 25 (28, 31) on back of sock (Heel) and 26 (28, 30) sts on front of sock (Instep).

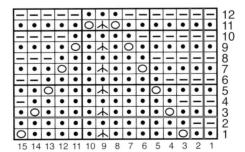

15 14 13 12 11 10 9 8 7 6 5 4 3 2 1

Chart 1

Work the entire chart for size extra large only. Work from the red line across for size large. Work inside the blue lines for size small/medium (begin on Rnd 3 for size small/medium).

HEEL FLAP

Work on 25 (28, 31) Heel sts. Place rem 26 (28, 30) sts on hold for Instep.

Row 1 (WS): *K1, p2; rep from * to last st, k1.

Row 2: *P1, k1, yo, k1; rep from * to last st, p1.

Row 3: *K1, p3; rep from * to last st, k1.

Row 4: *P1, sl 1, k2, psso; rep from * to last st, p1.

Rep Rows 1–4 5 (5, 6) more times. On last row, inc 1 (0, 0) st and dec 0 (1, 1) sts—26 (27, 30) sts.

TURN HEEL

Row 1 (RS): K16 (17, 19), ssk, turn.

Row 2: Sl 1, p6 (7, 8), p2tog, turn.

Row 3: Sl 1, k6 (7, 8), ssk, turn.

Rep Rows 2–3 until all sts have been worked—8 (9, 10) sts. Purl 1 row.

GUSSET

Pick up and knit 12 (13, 14) sts along side of Heel Flap, knit across Instep sts, pick up and knit 12 (13, 14) sts along opposite side of Heel Flap, knit to beg of Instep sts, dec 0 (1, 0) sts across Heel—58 (62, 68) sts.

Rnd 1: Knit across Instep sts; on sole sts work k1, ssk, knit to last 3 sts, k2tog, k1.

Rnd 2: Knit.

Rep Rnds 1–2 until 50 (54, 58) sts rem—26 (28, 30) Instep sts and 24 (26, 28) Heel sts. Work even until piece measures 2" (5cm) less than desired length.

TOE

Set-up Rnd: On Instep work k1, ssk, knit to last 3 sts, k2tog, k1; knit all Heel sts.

Rnd 1: On Instep work k1, ssk, knit to last 3 sts, k2tog, k1; rep on Heel sts.

Rnd 2: Knit.

Rep Rnds 1–2 until 16 (16, 16) sts rem.

FINISHING

Graft Toe using Kitchener stitch. Weave in ends.

Stalking Socks and Anklets

These socks use the same materials as the knee-highs. To create the anklets pictured, use the instructions on page 16 for converting a knee-high pattern to a short sock with a turnback cuff.

CUFF

Using long-tail cast on and larger needles, CO 52 (56, 60) sts. Join in a rnd, being careful not to twist sts. Purl 1 rnd, knit 1 rnd, purl 1 rnd. Work Chart 1 (page 103) a total of 3 times (2 times for anklet). Knit 1 rnd, purl 1 rnd. Change to smaller needles.

LEG

Turn work inside out for cuff turnback and cont as follows:

Work in p1, k2 rib for 1 rnd, dec 1 (2, 0) st evenly—51 (54, 60) sts.

Work in p1, k2 rib for 5 rnds.

Work in p1, k2 rib for 1 rnd, inc 0 (2, 1) sts—51 (56, 61) sts.

Pm 25 (28, 31) sts from beg of rnd to mark back of sock. Rem 26 (28, 30) sts are front of sock. Change to larger needles.

Rnd 1: *P1, k2; rep from * to 1 st before marker, p1, knit to end of rnd.

Rnd 2: *P1, k1, yo, k1; rep from * to 1 st before marker, p1, knit to end of rnd.

Rnd 3: *P1, k3; rep from * to 1 st before marker, p1, knit to end of rnd.

Rnd 4: *P1, sl 1, k2, psso; rep from * to 1 st before marker, p1, knit to end of rnd.

Rep Rnds 1–4 until piece from turnback measures 8" (20.5cm).

Finish Sock as for Knee-High from Heel Flap to Finishing.

The socks shown here were made using Briggs and Little Regal (100% wool, 4oz./113g, 272yd./249m) in color Forest Brown; the Anklets were made using color Briar Rose.

Omar's Carpet Knee-Highs

The patterns on these knee-highs are adapted from carpets, kilims and traditional socks from Turkey, Ukraine, Lebanon and many other sources. The heel treatment is one I "unvented" (to use Elizabeth Zimmerman's phrase)—the heel flap is done while still knitting in the round, so no stitches need to be picked up later. The shaping is done down the sides of the leg.

SIZES

Small/Medium (Large, Extra Large)

FINISHED MEASUREMENTS

To fit foot up to an 8½" (9", 9½") (21.5cm [23cm, 24cm]) circumference

YARN

2 (3½oz./100g, 212yd./194m) skeins DK weight yarn, 1 skein each of 2 colors (MC and CC)

The knee-highs shown here were made using Handwerks Super DK (100% superwash merino wool, 3½oz./100g, 212yd./194m) in colors Chamomile (MC) and Sumac (CC).

NEEDLES

Set of 5 US 4 (3.5mm) dpns or 2 circular needles, or size needed to obtain gauge

NOTIONS

Stitch markers

Yarn needle

GAUGE

13 sts = 2" (5cm) in patt, after blocking

Picot Cast On

*CO 4 sts using the knitted cast on. BO 2 sts, sl the rem st on the right-hand needle to the left-hand needle; rep from * until the desired number of sts are cast on.

LEG

Using Picot Cast On and MC, CO 72 (76, 80) sts. Join in a rnd, being careful not to twist sts. Purl side is RS.

Rnd 1: Knit.

Rnd 2: Purl.

Rnd 3: Knit.

Rnd 4: With CC, *k1, p1; rep from * around.

Rnd 5: With CC, *p1, k1; rep from * around.

Rnd 6: With MC, *k1, p1; rep from * around.

Rnd 7: With MC, *p1, k1; rep from * around.

Rnd 8: With CC, purl.

Rnds 9–19: With CC, *k1, p1; rep from * around.

Rnd 20: With MC, *p1, k1; rep from * around.

Rnd 21: With MC, purl.

Next rnd: *With CC, k1; work Rnd 1 of Chart 1 (page 108) over next 25 (27, 29) sts; with CC, k1, work Rnd 1 of Chart 2 (page 109) over next 9 sts; rep from * to end. Cont as established until piece measures 13" (33cm)—54 (58, 62) sts.

GUSSET

Work first 27 (29, 31) sts for Heel; rem 27 (29, 31) sts for Instep.

Note: The first inc st for Gusset Chart 1 (page 109) is done in the first st of the Heel Flap—knit into the front of the st with the inc color, knit into the back of the st with the Heel Flap color. The first inc st for Gusset Chart 2 (page 109) is done in the first st of the Instep—knit into the front of the st with the inc color, knit into the back of the st with the Instep color.

Next rnd: Work Rnd 1 of Gusset Chart 1; work across 27 (29, 31) Heel sts as established (with CC, k1; work Chart 1 as established; with CC, k1); work Rnd 1 of Gusset Chart 2; work Instep sts as established (with CC, k1; work Chart 1 as established; with CC, k1). Cont as established to A (B, C) on Gusset Charts—7 (8, 9) sts on each Gusset, 68 (74, 80) sts.

TURN HEEL

Work in stripe patt across 7 (8, 9) Gusset sts; across 27 (29, 31) Heel sts work k1 CC, k1 MC; wrap and turn, purl back across Heel sts; with CC, inc 1 (1, 1) st—28 (30, 32) sts. Wrap and turn.

With CC, cont in rows on these 28 (30, 32) sts:

Row 1 (RS): K14, ssk, k1, turn.

Row 2: Sl 1, p1, p2tog, p1, turn.

Row 3: Sl 1, k2, ssk, k1, turn.

Row 4: Sl 1, p3, p2tog, p1, turn.

Cont in this manner, working 1 more st before dec each row until all sts have been worked—14 (16, 16) sts; 28 (32, 34) total Heel sts (including Gussets).

Next rnd: Sl 1, knit across 14 (16, 16) Heel sts. Knit Gusset, Instep, and Gusset in patt, knitting last st tog with first—27 (31, 33) Heel sts, 27 (29, 31) Instep sts. Next rnd, dec 0 (2, 2) sts evenly across Heel sts—54 (58, 62) total sts. Work even in patt until piece measures 2" (5cm) less than desired length.

TOE

With CC, knit 1 rnd. Follow appropriate Toe Chart for your size (page 110) across Instep and Heel sts, working dec in CC—22 (26, 30) sts. With CC, knit 1 rnd.

FINISHING

Graft Toe using Kitchener stitch. Weave in ends.

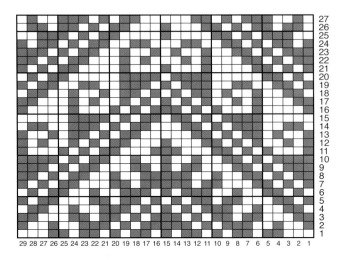

Chart 1

Knit the full chart for size extra large only. For size large, omit stitches 1 and 29. For size small/medium, omit stitches 1, 2, 28 and 29.

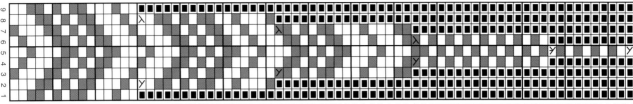

Chart 2 (chart rotated to fit page)

Special Symbol

☐ knit in the front and back of the same stitch—1 st inc

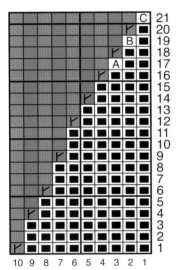

Gusset Chart 1

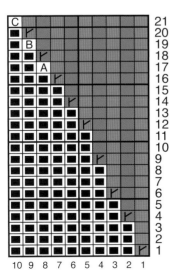

Gusset Chart 2

109

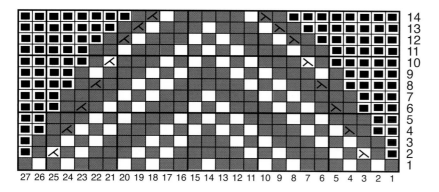

Toe Chart (Size Small/Medium)

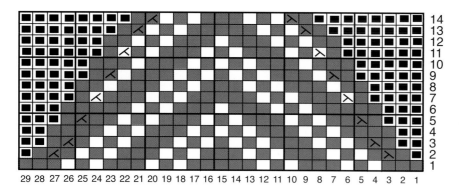

Toe Chart (Size Large)

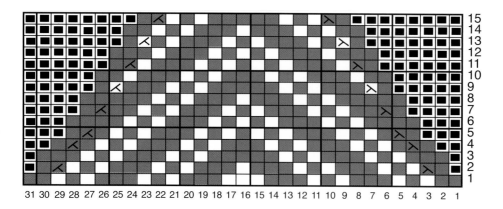

Toe Chart (Size Extra Large)

Omar's Carpet Socks

These socks use the same materials as the knee-highs, but a change in color makes the pattern more subtle.

LEG

Using Picot Cast On (see page 107) and MC, CO 54 (58, 62) sts. Join in a rnd, being careful not to twist sts. Purl side is RS.

Rnd 1: Knit.

Rnd 2: Purl.

Rnd 3: Knit.

Rnd 4: With CC, *k1, p1; rep from * around.

Rnd 5: With CC, *p1, k1; rep from * around.

Rnd 6: With MC, *k1, p1; rep from * around.

Rnd 7: With MC, *p1, k1; rep from * around.

Rnd 8: With CC, purl.

Rnds 9–19: With CC, work in k1, p1 rib.

Rnd 20: With MC, *p1, k1; rep from * around.

Rnd 21: With MC, purl.

Next rnd: *With CC, k1; work Rnd 1 of Chart 1 (page 108) over next 25 (27, 29) sts; with CC, k2, work Rnd 1 of Chart 1 once more, with CC, k1. Cont as established until piece measures 8" (20.5cm) or desired length. Finish Sock as for Knee-High from Gusset to Finishing.

The knee-highs shown here were made using Handwerks Super DK (100% superwash merino wool, 3¹/₂oz./100g, 212yd./194m) in colors Mulberry (MC) and Sumac (CC).

Mary Wilson's Gift Knee-Highs

Mary Wilson, a member of the Quw'utsun' Band on Vancouver Island, gave woven cedar baskets as gifts to her adopted sister, my great-grandmother Jeremina Colvin. They are still treasured in our family. This pattern is adapted from designs on those cedar baskets, which were woven at the beginning of the 20th century.

The colors used in these knee-highs are a reflection of the natural shades used in Native weavings; these shades came from dyes made using plants that grew nearby. The shaping on this pair of knee-highs is worked in a panel down the back.

SIZE

Small/Medium (Large, Extra Large)

FINISHED MEASUREMENTS

To fit foot up to an 8¼" (8¾", 9") (21cm [22cm, 23cm]) circumference

YARN

6 (1¾oz./50g, 150yd./137m) skeins sport weight yarn; 3 skeins MC, 2 skeins CC1 and 1 skein CC2

The knee-highs shown here were made using St. Denis/Classic Elite Nordique (100% wool, 1¾oz./50g, 150yd./137m) in colors #5897 Olive (MC), #5815 Emerald (CC1) and #5821 Sage (CC2).

NEEDLES

Set of 5 US 2 (2.75mm) dpns or 2 circular needles, or size needed to obtain gauge

Set of 5 dpns or 2 circular needles 1 size smaller

NOTIONS

Stitch markers

Yarn needle

GAUGE

15 sts = 2" (5cm) in patt, after blocking

Leg

With smaller needles and CC1, CO 84 (87, 90) sts. Join in a rnd, being careful not to twist sts. Work in k2, p1 rib for 2" (5cm). Change to larger needles and knit 1 rnd, inc 0 (1, 2) sts—84 (88, 92) sts. Follow appropriate Chart 1 for your size, working all rnds once.

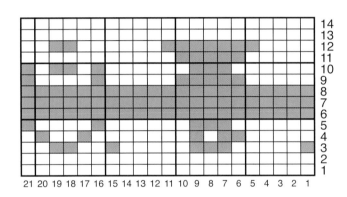

Chart 1 (Size Small/Medium)

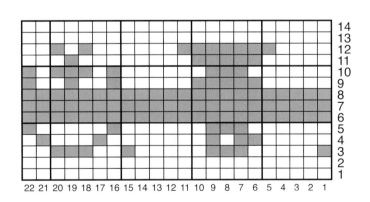

Chart 1 (Size Large)

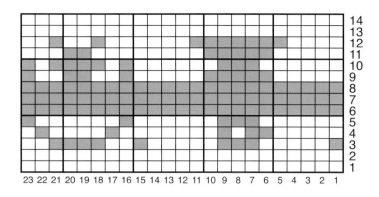

Chart 1 (Size Extra Large)

Next rnd: With MC, *k1, p1; rep from * around. With CC2, knit 1 rnd.

Next rnd: With MC, *p1, k1; rep from * around. With CC2, knit 1 rnd, dec 0 (0, 2) sts—84 (88, 90) sts. Cont as follows:

Size small/medium: Work Chart 2 (Size Small/Medium) (page 115) over 12 sts, work Shaping Chart over next 32 sts, rep Chart 3 (Size Small/Medium) (page 115) to end.

Size large: Work Chart 2 (Size Large) (page 115) over 12 sts, work Shaping Chart over next 32 sts, rep Chart 3 (Size Large) (page 115) to end.

Size extra large: Work Chart 2 (Size Extra Large) (page 115) over 12 sts, work Shaping Chart over next 32 sts, rep Chart 3 (Size Extra Large) (page 115) to end.

Work even in patt until piece measures 13" (33cm)—62 (66, 68) sts.

Heel Flap

Move first 1 (1, 2) sts of rnd to end. Next 31 (33, 34) sts are worked for Heel Flap. Place rem 31 (33, 34) sts on hold for Instep. With MC, knit across Heel sts, inc 1 (1, 0) st—32 (34, 34) sts.

Slide work back to beg of needle. With CC1, *sl, k1; rep from * across.

Row 1 (WS): Both yarns are now at same end of needle. With MC, *sl 1, p1; rep from * across.

Row 2 (WS): Slide work back to beg of needle. With CC1, purl.

Row 3 (RS): Both yarns are now at same end of needle. With MC, *sl 1, k1; rep from * across.

Row 4 (RS): Slide work back to beg of needle. With CC1, knit.

Rep Rows 1–4 a total of 6 (7, 7) times, then work Rows 1–2 once more. Break off MC.

Shaping Chart

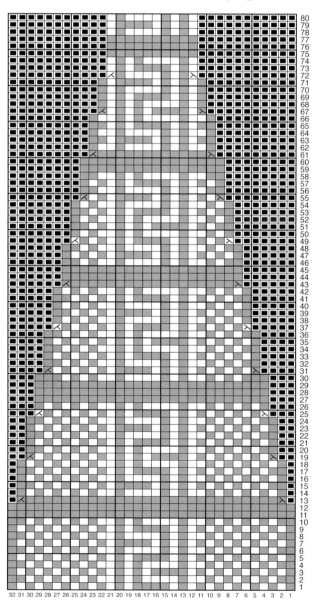

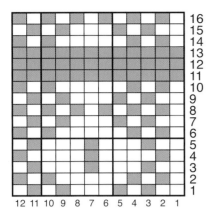

Chart 2 (Size Small/Medium)

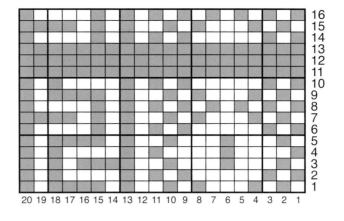

Chart 3 (Size Small/Medium)

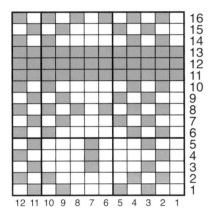

Chart 2 (Size Large)

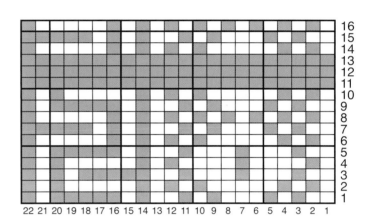

Chart 3 (Size Large)

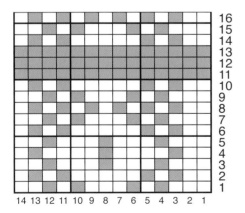

Chart 2 (Size Extra Large)

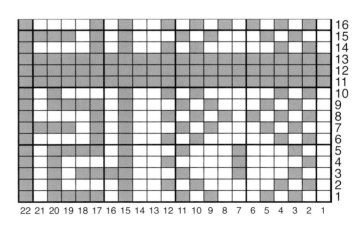

Chart 3 (Size Extra Large)

Turn Heel

Row 1 (RS): K16 (17, 17), ssk, k1, turn.

Row 2: Sl 1, p1, p2tog, p1, turn.

Row 3: Sl 1, k2, ssk, k1, turn.

Row 4: Sl 1, p3, p2tog, p1, turn.

Cont in this manner, working 1 more st before dec each row until all sts have been worked—16 (18, 18) sts. Break yarn.

Gusset

With MC, pick up and knit 14 (15, 16) sts along side of Heel Flap. Knit across Heel sts, inc 1 (1, 1) st. Pick up and knit 14 (15, 16) sts along opposite side of Heel flap—45 (49, 51) Heel sts.

Rnd 1: Work in established patt across Instep sts, *with CC, k1; with MC, k1; rep from * across Heel sts.

Rnd 2: Work in patt across Instep sts, on Heel sts, with CC, ssk; work in stripe patt to last 2 sts, with CC, k2tog.

Rep Rnds 1–2 until 35 (37, 39) Heel sts rem, maintaining stripe patt and Instep patt. Work even in patt until piece measures 2½" (6.5cm) less than desired length. Dec 0 (0, 1) sts on Heel on last rnd—66 (70, 72) sts.

Toe

With MC, knit 1 rnd.

Next rnd: *With MC, k1; with CC, k1; rep from * around.

Rnds 1–2: With MC, k2; knit across Instep, working opposite color in each st as worked on previous row to last 2 sts, with MC, k2. On Heel sts, work with MC, k1, ssk; work as for Instep to last 3 sts, with MC, k2tog, k1—62 (66, 68) sts.

Rnd 3: With MC, k2; knit in check patt as set to last 2 sts of Instep, with MC, k2; rep across Heel sts.

Rnd 4: With MC, k1, ssk; work in patt to last 3 sts, with MC, k2tog, k1; rep across Heel sts.

Rep Rnds 3–4 until 30 (30, 34) sts rem. Rep Rnd 4 until 26 (26, 30) sts rem.

Finishing

Graft Toe using Kitchener stitch. Weave in ends.

Mary Wilson's Gift Socks and Legwarmers

The socks and legwarmers shown here use colors inspired by modern designs created after aniline dyes became available, as opposed to the natural shades shown in the knee-highs. To create the legwarmers pictured, use the instructions on page 17 for converting a knee-high pattern to a legwarmer pattern. Please note that the socks vary from the knee-highs in both the finished measurements and the amount of yarn used.

FINISHED MEASUREMENTS

To fit foot up to an 8½" (9", 9½") (21.5cm [23cm, 24cm]) circumference

YARN

5 (1¾oz./50g, 150yd./137m) skeins sport weight yarn; 2 skeins MC, 2 skeins CC1 and 1 skein CC2

LEG

With smaller needles and CC1, CO 63 (66, 69) sts. Join in a rnd, being careful not to twist sts. Work in k2, p1 rib for 2" (5cm). Change to larger needles and knit 1 rnd. Follow appropriate Chart 1 (pages 113–114), working all rnds once. Dec 1 (0, 1) st on last rnd—62 (66, 68) sts.

Next rnd: With MC, *k1, p1; rep from * around. With CC2, knit 1 rnd.

Next rnd: With MC, *p1, k1; rep from * around. With CC2, knit 1 rnd, inc 1 (0, 1) sts—63 (66, 69) sts.

Follow appropriate Chart 3 for your size (page 115) until piece measures 7" (18cm) or desired length. Dec 1 (0, 1) st in last rnd. Finish Sock as for Knee-High from Heel Flap to Finishing.

The socks and legwarmers shown here were made using St. Denis/Classic Elite Nordique (100% wool, 1¾oz./50g, 150yd./137m) in colors #5813 Black (MC), #5858 Red (CC1) and #5801 White (CC2).

Dance Little Jean Knee-Highs

These socks were inspired by the song "Dance Little Jean" by Nitty Gritty Dirt Band:
"When suddenly from out of nowhere a little girl came dancing 'cross the floor.
All her crinolines were billowing beneath the skirt of calico that she wore…"

These seemed like the perfect socks for Little Jean to be wearing as she danced. The shaping is done in a panel of stitches down the back. The eyelets running between the cables give these more stretch than you'd usually find in cabled knee-highs, making them easier to fit to the leg.

SIZE

Small/Medium (Large, Extra Large)

FINISHED MEASUREMENTS

To fit foot up to an 8" (9", 10¼") (20.5cm [23cm, 26cm]) circumference

YARN

6 (7, 7) (1¾oz./50g, 109yd./100m) skeins sport weight yarn; 4 (5, 5) skeins MC, 1 skein each CC1 and CC2.

The knee-highs shown here were made using Dale Heilo (100% wool, 1¾oz./50g, 109yd./100m) in colors #20 Natural (MC), #4018 Cherry Red (CC1) and #90 Black (CC2).

NEEDLES

Set of 5 US 3 (3mm) dpns or 2 circular needles, or size needed to obtain gauge

NOTIONS

Cable needle
Stitch markers
Yarn needle

GAUGE

14 sts = 2" (5cm) in patt, after blocking

LEG

Using long-tail cast on and CC1, CO 78 (84, 90) sts.

Knit 1 rnd. Join in a rnd, being careful not to twist sts. Join MC.

Rnd 1: *K5, sl 1 wyib; rep from * around.

Rnd 2: *P5, sl 1 wyib; rep from * around (to sl 1 wyib, bring yarn between needles to back of work, sl 1, bring yarn back to front of work).

Rep Rnds 1–2 a total of 3 times, then work Rnd 1 once more.

Knit 1 rnd. Work 9 rnds of k1, p1 rib. Knit 2 rnds.

Join CC2.

Next rnd: *With MC, p1; with CC2, p1; rep from * around. Always bring new yarn up from underneath last yarn used.

Next rnd: *With MC, k1; with CC2, k1; rep from * around.

With MC, knit 4 rnds. Work Chart 1.

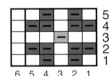

Chart 1

Special Symbol

⊟ carry 2 strands of CC1 or CC2 in front of st

With MC, knit 4 rnds.

Next rnd: *With MC, k1; with CC2, k1; rep from * around.

Next rnd: *With MC, p1; with CC2, p1; rep from * around. Always bring new yarn up from underneath last yarn used.

With MC, knit 2 rnds, dec 2 (0, 0) and inc 0 (0, 2) sts in the first rnd—76 (84, 92) sts. Pm after 56 (64, 72) sts to mark 20-st shaping area.

Work Rnd 1 of Chart 2 (page 120) on first 56 (64, 72) sts, work Rnd 1 of Shaping Chart (page 120) on next 20 sts. Work as established until piece measures 13" (33cm), ending with Rnd 10 or Rnd 20. For the last dec in shaping, when 4 sts rem in shaping, work k2, k2tog, then k2tog at end of rnd. After last rnd of Shaping Chart, when 2 shaping sts rem, at beg of rnd work sl 1, k2tog, psso to remove last shaping sts—56 (64, 72) sts. Move this st to end of rnd. Break off MC.

Special Symbols

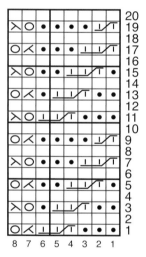

sl 1 to cable needle to back, k1, k1 from cable needle

sl 1 to cable needle to front, k1, k1 from cable needle

sl 1 to cable needle to back, k2, k1 from cable needle

sl 2 to cable needle to front, k1, k2 from cable needle

Chart 2

Shaping Chart

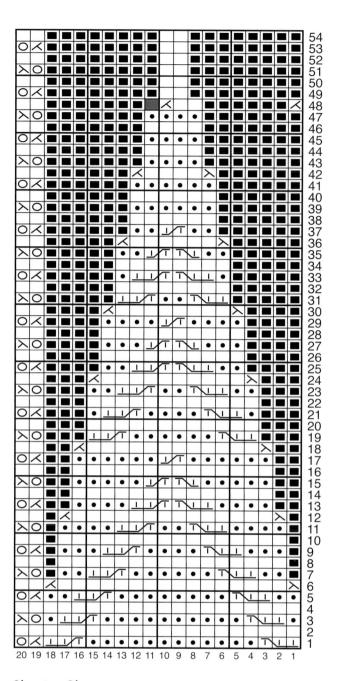

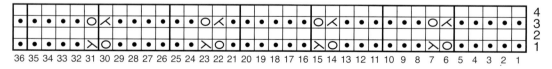

Instep Chart

Work the full chart for size extra large only. For size large, omit stitches 1, 2, 35 and 36. For size small/medium, omit stitches 1–4 and 33–36.

Heel Flap

Work Heel Flap on first 13 (11, 9) and last 15 (21, 27) sts of rnd. Place rem 28 (32, 36) sts on hold for Instep. Join CC2.

Row 1 (RS): Purl.

Row 2: Sl 1, knit to end. Break off CC2.

Row 3: Join CC1, *sl 1, k1; rep from * to end of row.

Row 4: Sl 1, purl to end of row. Break off CC1.

Row 5: Join MC, *sl 1, k1; rep from * to end of row.

Row 6: Sl 1, purl to end of row.

Rep Rows 5–6 11 (12, 13) times more.

Turn Heel

Row 1 (RS): K14 (16, 18), ssk, k1, turn.

Row 2: Sl 1, p1, p2tog, p1, turn.

Row 3: Sl 1, k2, ssk, k1, turn.

Cont in this manner, working 1 more st before dec each row until all sts have been worked—14 (16, 18) sts.

Gusset

Knit across Heel sts. Pick up and knit 15 (16, 17) sts along side of Heel Flap. Work Instep Chart (page 120) across 28 (32, 36) Instep sts, beg with Rnd 1 if leg ended on Rnd 10 and beg with Rnd 3 if leg ended on Rnd 20. Pick up and knit 15 (16, 17) sts along opposite side of Heel Flap—72 (80, 88) sts. Knit to center of Heel.

Rnd 1: Work even in patt.

Rnd 2: Knit to last 3 Heel sts, k2tog, k1; work Instep sts in patt; k1, ssk knit to end.

Rep Rnds 1–2 until 56 (64, 72) sts rem. Work even until piece measures 2¼" (5.5cm) less than desired length, ending with Rnd 2 or 4 of Instep Chart.

Toe

Rnd 1: Join CC2, *sl 1, k1; rep from * around. Break yarn.

Rnd 2: Join CC1, knit. Break yarn.

Rnd 3: Join MC, *k1, sl 1; rep from * around.

Rnd 4: Knit.

Rnd 5: Knit to last 3 Heel sts, k2tog, k1; on Instep work k1, ssk, work to last 3 sts, k2tog, k1; k1, ssk, knit to end of rnd.

Rep Rnds 4–5 until 28 (32, 36) sts rem. Rep Rnd 5 until 16 sts rem.

Finishing

Graft Toe using Kitchener stitch. Weave in ends.

Dance Little Jean Socks

These socks, adapted from the knee-high pattern, are good for dancing, as well! The amount of yarn used varies from the knee-highs.

YARN

5 (6, 6) (1¾oz./50g, 109yd./100m) skeins sport weight yarn; 3 (4, 4) skeins MC, 1 skein each CC1 and CC2

Leg

Using long-tail cast on and CC1, CO 54 (60, 66) sts. Knit 1 rnd. Join in a rnd, being careful not to twist sts. Join MC.

Rnd 1: *K5, sl 1 wyib; rep from * around.

Rnd 2: *P5, sl 1 wyib; rep from * around (to sl 1 wyib, bring yarn between needles to back of work, sl 1, bring yarn back to front of work). Rep Rnds 1–2 a total of 3 times, then work Rnd 1 once more.

Knit 1 rnd. Work 9 rnds of k1, p1 rib. Knit 2 rnds. Join CC2.

Next rnd: *With MC, p1; with CC2, p1; rep from * around. Always bring new yarn up from underneath last yarn used.

Next rnd: *With MC, k1; with CC2, k1; rep from * around.

With MC, knit 4 rnds. Work Chart 1 (page 119).

With MC, knit 4 rnds.

Next rnd: *With MC, k1; with CC2, k1; rep from * around.

Next rnd: *With MC, p1; with CC2, p1; rep from * around. Always bring new yarn up from underneath last yarn used.

With MC, knit 2 rnds, inc 2 (4, 6) sts in the first rnd—56 (64, 72) sts. Work Chart 2 (page 120) until piece measures 8" (20.5cm) or desired length, ending with Rnd 10 or 20. Break off MC. Finish Sock as for Knee-High from Heel Flap to Finishing.

The socks shown here were made using Dale Heilo (100% wool, 1¾oz./50g, 109yd./100m) in colors #4 Sand Heather (MC), #4018 Cherry Red (CC1) and #90 Black (CC2).

General Knitting Information

Yarn Weight Guidelines

Since the names given to different weights of yarn can vary widely depending on the country of origin or the yarn manufacturer's preference, the Craft Yarn Council of America has put together a standard yarn weight system to impose a bit of order on the sometimes unruly yarn labels. Look for a picture of a skein of yarn with a number 0–6 on most kinds of yarn to figure out its "official" weight. The information in the chart below is taken from www.yarnstandards.com.

	Super Bulky (6)	Bulky (5)	Medium (4)	Light (3)	Fine (2)	Superfine (1)	Lace (0)
Weight	super-chunky, bulky, roving	chunky, craft, rug	worsted, afghan, aran	light worsted, DK	sport, baby, 4ply	sock, fingering, 2ply, 3ply	fingering, 10-count crochet thread
Knit Gauge Range*	6–11 sts	12–15 sts	16–20 sts	21–24 sts	23–26 sts	27–32 sts	33–40 sts
Recommended Needle Range**	11 (8mm) and larger	9 to 11 (5.5–8mm)	7 to 9 (4.5–5.5mm)	5 to 7 (3.75–4.5mm)	3 to 5 (3.25–3.75mm)	1 to 3 (2.25–3.25mm)	000 to 1 (2–2.25mm)

Notes: * Gauge (tension) is measured over 4" (10cm) in Stockinette (stocking) stitch.

         ** US needle sizes are given first, with UK equivalents in brackets.

Substituting Yarns

If you substitute yarn, be sure to select a yarn of the same weight as the yarn recommended for the project. Even after checking that the recommended gauge on the yarn you plan to substitute is the same as for the yarn listed in the pattern, make sure to knit a swatch to ensure that the yarn and needles you are using will produce the correct gauge and stretch.

In the instructions for the projects, I have favored US knitting terms. Refer to this box for the UK equivalent.

US Term	UK Term
bind off	cast off
gauge	tension
Stockinette stitch	stocking stitch
reverse Stockinette stitch	reverse stocking stitch
seed stitch	moss stitch
moss stitch	double moss stitch

Knitting Needle Sizes

US	Metric
0	2mm
1	2.25mm
1½	2.5mm
2	2.75mm
2½	3mm
3	3.25mm
4	3.5mm
5	3.75mm
6	4mm
7	4.5mm
8	5mm
9	5.5mm
10	6mm
10½	6.5mm
	7mm
	7.5mm
11	8mm
13	9mm
15	10mm
17	12.75mm
19	15mm
35	19mm
36	20mm

Abbreviations

beg	begin, beginning
CO	cast on
cont	continue, continuing
dec	decrease
dpn(s)	double-pointed needles
est	established
foll	follow(ing)
inc	increase
k	knit
k2tog	knit 2 together
p	purl
pm	place marker
psso	pass slipped stitch over
p2sso	pass 2 slipped stitches over
rem	remaining
RS	right side
rnd	round
rep	repeat
sl	slip
sm	slip marker
ssk	slip, slip, knit
st(s)	stitch(es)
tog	together
WS	wrong side
wyib	with yarn in back
wyif	with yarn in front
yo	yarn over

Symbol Key

● or ☐	knit
⊟	purl
⊙	yarn over
⊠	knit 2 together
⊡	purl 2 together
⊠	slip, slip, knit
⊼	slip 2 together knitwise, knit 1, pass 2 slipped stitches over
⊠	slip 1 stitch knitwise, knit 2, pass slipped stitch over
■	no stitch

Resources

Yarn

Black Bunny Fibers
http://shop.blackbunnyfibers.com

Blue Moon Fiber Arts
http://www.bluemoonfiberarts.com/newmoon

Briggs & Little
http://briggsandlittle.com/wool

Clever Yarn
http://www.cleveryarn.com

Handwerks Artisan Yarns & Textiles
http://handwerkstextiles.com

Knit Witch
http://knitwitch.com

Prairie Fibre Mill Inc.
Box 1539, Biggar, Saskatchewan. S0K 0M0
306-882-4542
themill@sasktel.net

Schoolhouse Press
http://schoolhousepress.com

Shelridge Farm
http://shelridge.com

St Denis
www.stdenisyarns.com/shop/home.php

Three Irish Girls
http://www.threeirishgirls.com

Uptown Stitches
http://www.uptownstitches.com

Van Der Rock Yarns
http://www.vanderrockyarns.com

Wool2Dye4
http://wool2dye4.com/catalog/index.php

Knitting Needles

DyakCraft
www.dyakcraft.com/needles.htm

HiyaHiya Worldwide
www.hiyahiya.com/needle_1.html

Website

www.thedietdiary.com/knittingfiend/tools/
EstimatingYardageSock.html

Books

Knitting Socks with Handpainted Yarn
Carol Sulcoski
(Interweave Press)

Designs for Knitting Kilt Hose
Lady Veronica Gainford
(Schoolhouse Press)

And A Time to Knit Stockings (electronic book on CD)
Katherine Misegades

Index

Still searching for more socks?

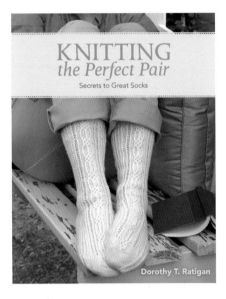

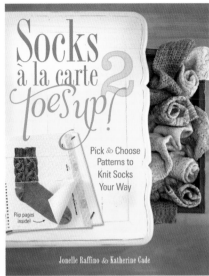